BUILDING STUDY SKILLS

Second Edition

WILLIAM L. CHRISTEN
LARRY L. WELCH
DEBRA J. ELLIOTT
KAREN J. ATWOOD

ILLUSTRATED BY *Chris Hackett*

**KENDALL/HUNT
PUBLISHING COMPANY**
Dubuque, Iowa

Cover photo by James L. Shaffer

Copyright © 1983, 1984 by Kendall/Hunt Publishing Company

ISBN 0–8403–3357–9

Printed in the United States of America
10 9 8 7 6 5 4 3 2 1

C   403357   01

Contents

To the Student

Building Study Skills is a book designed to help you develop and improve your reading and study skills. Throughout the book you will be introduced to new study strategies that will help you become a more efficient student. As we mention in Chapter 1 of the book, we want you to learn how to WORK SMARTER RATHER THAN HARDER!

In this book we will cover the following skills:

* *Establishing Good Study Habits*—Ways you can use to help you set up good study practices immediately.
* *Listening Skills*—Ways on how to listen for important ideas in the classes you are taking and how to ask good questions.
* *Vocabulary Development*—Ways to improve your vocabulary skills in reading, writing, and listening.
* *Finding the Main Idea*—Ways to learn how to find the main idea and the supporting details in reading and listening.
* *Notetaking*—A system of notetaking that will aid you in recording good information from your reading and in your classes.
* *Mapping*—A way of taking notes or other written information and making a "picture" of the information.
* *Time Management*—Ways of planning your time in and out of school.
* *Test Taking/Preparation*—Ways to get ready for tests as well as what to do in the test itself.
* *Memory Techniques*—Some hints on how to remember important information and how to store it in long-term memory.
* *Reading Comprehension Selections*—Readings and vocabulary exercises around the content areas to help you become a more effective reader.
* *Rate Boost Readings*—Practice in reading to improve your reading rate (speed) showing you that you can change your reading rate from subject to subject.

By completing the material in this book and by implementing this in your daily school life, you are on your way to becoming a more successful student! We know from working with thousands of students the study skills presented in this book will increase your ability to learn. We want you to make a total effort to learn and use these skills. If you do, you will reach your highest potential as a student. Good luck as you begin your journey through this book!

WLC
LLW
DJE
KJA

Acknowledgments

Many people worked hard to make this book possible. The authors would like to thank the following people who contributed to the development and writing of these materials: Patricia Apraham, Deer Valley School District; Barbara Dickerson, Doctoral Student-Arizona State University; Barbara Dalicandro, Deer Valley School District; Connie Harris, Deer Valley School District; Michael Lang, Mesa Public School District; Richard Malena, Doctoral Student-Arizona State University; Sharen Kellogg, Mesa Public School District; Hollis Sherman, Washington School District; Lynn Simon, Paradise Valley School District; Claire Sibold, Doctoral Student-Arizona State University; Claire Rottenberg, Tempe Elementary School District; Gerri Fiedler, Glendale Community College; Quana Fredicks, Scottsdale Public School District; and Nancy Welch, Governor's Office, State of Arizona.

Chapter 1
Getting Ready to Study

Did you realize that to be a good student requires determination, time, effort, and hard work? The question you should ask yourself is *Do I want to be a good student?* If the answer is yes, what can you do to become a more effective student? You can:

* Decide you want to learn what you are studying. (Motivation)
* Keep yourself tuned in to your work. (Concentration)
* Ask yourself questions as you read. (Active Reading)
* See how the pieces fit together. (Organization)
* Understand what you are reading. (Comprehension)
* Get new information into a usable form. (Notetaking/Mapping)
* Use the information you learned in your daily life. (Application)

These study skills, when used on a regular basis, will help you improve your learning. In this book you will learn how to work SMARTER RATHER THAN HARDER!

The remainder of this book is devoted to showing you how to use a variety of study skills. We hope you will work hard at learning these study skills and that you will use them on a regular basis in all of your classes!

What Study Habits Do You Have Now?

Let's take a few minutes to see how well you are doing right now. Many students believe they have good study habits. Yet many of them find it difficult to complete assignments on time or to get started on assignments. Consequently, they turn work in late or sometimes not at all.

Turn to page 1 in your *Student Activity Booklet*. Complete Activity 1.1, "Study Skills Questionnaire." Your teacher will give you directions.

What Are Some Instant Skills You Can Use?

To get you thinking about specific study skills, we thought we would show you some things you can use immediately. Each one can be done without any extra work on your part. They are:

(1) *Review your class notes regularly.* Before going to class, it is important to review the previous day's notes. This helps you get ready for the information of the new day. The more often you review your notes, the more likely you will store the information in long-term memory.

(2) *Write down everything the teacher writes on the chalkboard.* If the teacher takes time to write something on the chalkboard, it must be important. It will most likely appear on the next test. So, write the information from the chalkboard in your class notes.

(3) *Find one place to study at home.* It is very important to have a quiet place to study. To be able to concentrate on your work, you need a place that is free from distractions, well lighted, and comfortable. Several surveys show that 80% of all students use their bedroom for studying. If this is your place to study, make it a place where you can accomplish your study goals.

(4) *Determine the amount of time you will spend on each subject.* Before you start an assignment, write down the amount of time you think you will need to complete the work. By doing this you are setting a time goal for yourself. Work to meet that time goal. Keep a record sheet to see how well you do. As you get better at estimating your study time, you will find yourself using less time to finish your school work.

(5) *If your mind begins to wander, stop!* Sitting at a desk unable to concentrate is something we all experience. But don't let this take over your study time. If you find yourself daydreaming, stop, stand up and turn around. This physical act helps you recognize you are daydreaming. It will help you get yourself back to your study session. Try it! It works!

(6) *Reviewing your work is a smart investment.* Few students realize the value of short, regular reviews. By taking a few minutes on a regular basis to review your school work, you will have a better chance of getting it into long-term memory. So, review your work immediately after completing an assignment. Next, review it on a weekly basis. The immediate review will pay off.

How Should You Use This Book?

Before using any book, it is important to take time to discover what is in the book. By having advanced knowledge about what is in a book, you can use the book to your advantage. Use the following form as a guideline for learning more about this book. It will also help you preview other textbooks you have.

Turn to page 3 in your *Student Activity Booklet* and complete Activity 1.2.

Why Should You Complete Activities in This Textbook?

We urge you to complete all the activities in this book. By working through the activities you will begin to experience "how to" use the various skills being presented. It is equally important to begin using these skills regularly in all of your classes. Unless you work with each skill repeatedly, the skill most likely will be lost.

How Do You Learn New Information?

What are the ways you learn new material? If we were to ask you how you learn new information being taught in your classes, what would you say? Let's try to answer this question. On a sheet of paper or in your notebook, write down at least two ways you seem to learn new material.

Did you use the term *memory, memorize,* or *memorization?* Many people might say memory and learning are close to being the same. We'd like to have you look at memory and learning in a different way.

What Is Short-term Memory?

We would like you to think of short-term memory as the first place information goes in your mind. You might even think of it as a "sorting box." If nothing is done with the information at this time, it will be sorted out and lost. Short-term memory is not a permanent storage place. Once the new information is sorted, one of two things will happen:

1) if there is an intent to remember and/or the new information is linked to something already known, the information becomes part of long-term memory; or,
2) the new information is lost after a few moments.

To prevent the material being lost, you should make a record of this information. We call this notetaking. More will be discussed in Chapter 5 about notetaking.

Cramming is an example of trying to store information in working memory. Often students attempt to place many facts in their working memory to get ready for a test. During the exam, and certainly after the exam, most of the information remembered for the test will be lost. You are taking a chance putting information in working memory, especially if you want to recall it later.

What Is Long-term Storage?

This can be looked at as a "computer bank." Much like a computer, you can place information in long-term storage virtually forever. Then, when you need the information, you can retrieve it. The goal is to get new information into long-term storage.

There are several ways that will help you accomplish this goal. First, you need to become an *active learner*. You need to (1) have a purpose and intent to learn, (2) relate new information to things you already know, (3) organize new information into meaningful categories, and (4) use the various study skills you will learn. All of these strategies will help you get new information into long-term storage.

How Do You Motivate Yourself to Study and Learn?

Finding motivation to do school work is a problem for many students. Often times students put things off to the last minute. This usually results in unacceptable work.

Lack of personal motivation can be a serious problem. No one can give you personal motivation. This comes from within you. But we can give you some hints on how to become a motivated person.

First, *set learning goals for yourself.* Realistic goal setting gives you direction and purpose for your school work. By understanding what you need to do, you can motivate yourself to reach the goals you have set. Don't leave your school work to chance!

Second, *see how you can use the new information you study in your daily life.* If it has immediate application in your life, you will be more motivated to learn it. A good example of wanting to learn something new is getting your driver's license. No one really has to motivate you to learn how to drive a car. You are motivated because you really see a purpose for getting a driver's license. Making a connection between practical application and learning is a powerfully motivating force.

Third, *see how the classes you are taking fit into your career plans.* Careful analysis of your career choice is important. By knowing your career choice, you can steer yourself to classes which will help you reach your career goal. Doing this will prevent you from choosing classes that might be boring to you. Having a career in mind can be a motivating force.

And fourth, *you need to motivate yourself from within.* The real desire to learn comes from you. Being positive about yourself, your future, and your school life will help you become self-motivated. Work hard, enjoy your outside activities, and reward yourself for doing a good job. All of these will lead to becoming a motivated person.

How Can I Concentrate on My School Work?

Dividing your attention between two things most likely will result in little being accomplished. Giving your full attention to one task at a time is vital. Daydreaming and distractions are hazards all students face. Overcoming this problem is a must! Building solid concentration habits takes work. It also requires that you do some planning. Let's take a look at some hints for helping you build good concentration habits. They are:

1. *Prepare to concentrate and set a goal.* Plan seriously to get down to your school work. Start with a goal in mind. Don't leave a study session to chance. Your goal may simply be to read Chapter 8 and take notes in the next 30 minutes. Don't go to a study session with the attitude that "if it works out, okay; if not, who cares!"

2. *Choose a quiet place to study.* Your surroundings will help you set the stage to concentrate. If there are outside distractions like a TV or radio making noise, you probably will have difficulty concentrating on your school work. Also, be sure to have all of your study material at hand. To find out you need something in the middle of your study session will break your concentration. Plan to make sure this does not happen.

3. *Allow for breaks.* Build in time to stop for a rest break. Get up, stretch, take a walk, get something to drink, or whatever. The main thing is to plan some time off on a regular basis. After studying for 30–45 minutes, take a 5–10 minute break. You will find you can concentrate better after you do this.

4. *Get actively involved with the material.* If you want to concentrate on your work, you need to get involved with it. Ask yourself questions, take notes, make a map, learn the new vocabulary being presented. By becoming actively involved with the material, you will do a better job of concentrating.

5. *Vary your study activities.* Don't spend hours on the same subject or assignment. After spending a reasonable amount of time on one subject, change to another one. It is better to work on one subject for a period of time, do something else, and then come back to the original material.

6. *Set a study time.* Setting a regular time to study is a must! By knowing you have set specific time aside each night to do your school work, you will be more in the mood to concentrate.

To concentrate on your school work you must be determined to not allow yourself to be distracted. Decide whether your study place is well suited for learning.

Turn to page 5 in your *Student Activity Booklet* and complete Activity 1.3.

How Do I Set Learning Goals for Myself?

What do you want to learn? This is the first question you need to ask yourself. The answer is a starting point for writing learning goals. What you want to get out of a class becomes your goal(s). What you do in class and out of class will determine whether or not you reach your goal(s). Here is how you set a goal:

Steps for Setting Goals

Answer the following questions:

1. What is my *goal* for this class?

2. What are the *resources* available to me to help me reach these goals?

3. What are the *parts* of my goals?

4. What are my desired *outcomes?*

5. What actually *happened?*

6. Can I *apply* what I learned from setting goals?

Possible Answers:

1. My goal is to get a better grade in science this grading term.

2. The resources available to me are my teacher and friends who are in the same class.

3. To get a good grade on quiz 3 and quiz 4.

4. I want to get a "B" in my science class this grading term.

5. I got an "A" this grading term.

6. I can apply goal setting techniques in other classes.

WHEN YOU ARE WRITING GOALS BE SURE TO KEEP THE FOLLOWING POINTS IN MIND:

1. Clearly define your goals. *Be specific.*
2. Make sure your goals are attainable. *Be realistic.*
3. Keep your goals positive. *Be positive.*
4. Update your goals on a regular basis. *Be progressive.*

Turn to page 7 in your *Student Activity Booklet* and complete Activity 1.4.

Summary

Throughout this chapter we have talked about several ways to become a more *active learner*. To become a successful student you must work hard, set goals, and work at getting new material into long-term storage. Thinking about new information, organizing new information, and using the various study skills presented in this book will help you store information in your computer bank. By taking the responsibility for your learning and motivating yourself, you will discover learning to be a challenge to be met and enjoyed!

Now that you have completed this chapter, take a few minutes to reflect on the material covered. Complete the checklist found on page 9 in your *Student Activity Booklet*. (Activity 1.5)

Chapter 2
Budgeting Your Time Wisely

Have you ever said to yourself, "I just don't have time to complete my homework," or "it's 9 o'clock and I'm only half way done with my assignment." Many students find themselves asking these and other questions about managing their time. Part of the problem may be caused by failing to plan enough study time. It is important to begin planning how to use your time now. Don't let your day or week slip by.

What is your SSQ on time budgeting? To find out your SSQ turn to page 11 in your *Student Activity Booklet* and complete the checklist. (Activity 2.0)

How Does Time Management Work?

Scheduling your day or week does not mean planning for every minute of that time. It is not to be rigid. Rather, your schedule is a tool to help you plan your time wisely. Trading time when an emergency comes up is to be expected. If this happens, trade some time you were going to do one activity with some free time.

To get involved with time management, there are several things you need to do. The first step in time management is to *analyze how you use your time now*. To do this ask yourself these questions:

1. How do I spend my time now?
2. Is it usually productive?
3. Did I waste some of my time?

How Do You Make a Daily Schedule?

To make your daily schedule, think about what you need to do that day. You know you have classes during the day and other activities which need to be scheduled such as practice after school or responsibilities at home. In addition, be sure to set time aside for eating, studying, and personal recreation. Your schedule might look something like Example 2.1 on the following page.

Notice on this daily schedule the student has arranged the day. There is time for getting up and getting ready for school, attending classes, practicing after school, getting home and having dinner, relaxing before studying, studying for a test and reading a chapter assignment in science. By planning out your day, you are organizing your time wisely. You are not leaving anything to chance! This is what time management is all about. You want to take chance out of your life and replace it with order.

Turn to page 13 in your *Student Activity Booklet* and complete Activity 2.1.

EXAMPLE 2.1   *My Schedule for Today*

7—8 am   Get Up--prepare for school--eat breakfast

8–9 am   Arrive at school by 8:30 Homeroom

9–10 am   Language Arts

10–11 am   Science

11–12 noon Social Studies

12–1 pm   Lunch--Go to library for 15 min.

1–2 pm   Math

2–3 pm   P.E.

3–4 pm   Practice

4–5 pm   Practice/Leave for home

5–6 pm   Get home and relax before supper

6–7 pm   Supper--help with dishes

7–8 pm   Favorite TV program

8–9 pm   Homework--study time

9–10 pm   Finish homework--get ready for bed

after 10 pm

ACTIVITY 2.2 To practice making out a daily schedule, read the following day in the life of David. He is a lawyer. His days are very busy. See if you can schedule David's time for this day.

David is a lawyer practicing in a large city. On Monday, April 12, he arrives at his office at 8:30. His secretary reminds him that Miss Davis is coming at 11:00 to discuss a personal matter that she would not divulge over the phone. Mrs. Good is coming at 10:00 to find out about the city and county's requirements for subdividing some of her land. And, David is due at the courthouse at 2:00 to defend a local youth for shoplifting.

David will need about forty-five minutes to organize his papers and make notes for the shoplifting case. He may need to remain at the courthouse until 3:30. It will take him about 20 minutes to drive to the courthouse. He will need 10 minutes to review the sub-division ordinances before meeting with Mrs. Good, which may take an hour. He usually takes a forty-five minute lunch hour. If possible he'd like to exercise 30 minutes before lunch at a next door spa.

David always carries a daily planner booklet with him to jot down future events and things to do. He usually lists his daily schedule on an index card. In the near future, David will need about four hours to complete the Johnson contract and about five to complete the Witzer contract. The Johnsons are to come in at 1:00 on Tuesday to sign the contract. His secretary will need an hour to type the contract. His only other appointment tomorrow will be with Mr. Yates at 10:30 to finalize a real estate transaction, which will require about thirty minutes with no advance preparation. David does not work beyond 5:30 pm and does not take work home except in emergencies. He normally begins work at 8:30 am.

Now, turn to page 15 in your *Student Activity Booklet* and complete Activity 2.2 and 2.3.

How Can You Schedule for a Week?

Planning for an entire week might seem impossible. It isn't! In fact, this will be important to you in your school life as well as later in your chosen career. To be able to manage longer periods of time is essential.

Have you ever considered how much time there is in a week? Most likely you haven't. Take a look at this example of one week of a typical student:

EXAMPLE 2.2   *Hours in a Week*

THERE ARE	168	hours in a week (7 days × 24 hrs.)
YOU SPEND ABOUT	− 30	hours in class a week (6 classes × 5 days)
	138	left over
YOU SLEEP	− 56	hours per week (8 hrs. a night)
	82	hours of awake time are left
IF YOU STUDY	− 30	hours per week (that's one hour of study time for each hour of class time)
YOU HAVE LEFT	52	hours to do what you want to do

That is more than 7 hours per day. What you do with your time is important. Planning your day, week, or month is a must!

How can you manage the 24 hours in each day? First, determine what your fixed commitments are, such as: classes, practice, meetings, club work, meals, study time, and personal time. These most likely will not change from day to day. Second, schedule the rest of the time as needed.

What Is the Most Difficult Time to Manage?

The most difficult time to arrange is your time after school. You can waste the time or use it to your advantage. Granted, you need time for fun and relaxation, but you will also need to budget for other events like studying, chores, and extra-curricular activities at school. By doing this, you will have enough freedom to do the things YOU want to do!

What Does a Weekly Schedule Look Like?

The following weekly schedule is a typical one for a student. Take a look at this example.

EXAMPLE 2.3   *Student Schedule*

TIME	SUN	MON	TUES	WED	THURS	FRI	SAT
6–7 am	Sleep	Get up for school				→	
7–8 am	Get up	Leave by 8 / Homeroom				→	
8–9 am		Language Arts				→	Get up
9–10 am	Church	Science				→	Chores
10–11 am		P. E.				→	
11–12		Lunch				→	
12–1 pm		Math				→	
1–2 pm		Social studies				→	
2–3 pm		Shop				→	
3–4 pm		Practice			→		
4–5 pm		Practice			→		
5–6 pm		Home / Supper			→	Go to game	
6–7 pm		Free Time T. V.			→		
7–8 pm	Study	Study			→		
8–9 pm	Study	Study			→		
9–10 pm	←	Ready for bed					
10–11 pm							

10

ACTIVITY 2.4   Read the following schedule. Imagine it is your schedule for next week. With the information provided, fill in a weekly schedule for yourself. Be sure to take into consideration study time, recreation time, eating, and sleeping.

The day begins at 7:00 am. You get up and get ready for school. Your homeroom class begins at 8:30 and lasts for 30 minutes. From 10:00–11:00 you have reading on M, W, F and P.E. on Tu, Th. From 1:00–2:00 you have science and from 9:00–10:00 you have language arts. Your lunch break is from 12:00–1:00. From 11:00–12:00 is math. At 3:15 you have a special meeting with club members until 4:30 on Th. You also have a dentist appointment on Monday at 4:15. Your mother will pick you up at home. On Friday afternoon at 4:00 you plan to attend the football game.

As you plan for this week you take a look at the assignments you were given last week. In order to make sure you plan for these, you take some time to put them on your calendar. In math you will have a chapter test on Wednesday. A short one page essay is due in language arts on Thursday and you will have a short quiz in social studies on Friday. You have been invited to a roller skating party Friday evening at 8:00 pm and you have accepted the invitation. On Saturday morning you have a music lesson at 9:30 for one hour. After the lesson, you plan to go shopping in the afternoon.

Turn to page 19 in your *Student Activity Booklet* and complete Activity 2.4.

Now ask yourself, did I allow for:

	Yes	*No*
1. Enough travel time to the dentist appointment?	_____	_____
2. At least 30 minutes of music practice each day?	_____	_____
3. Study time on Monday and Tuesday for my math test?	_____	_____
4. Time to complete my essay at least one day before it was due?	_____	_____
5. Study time to prepare for the social studies quiz on Friday?	_____	_____
6. Special time to go shopping on Saturday?	_____	_____
7. Study time each night and on Sunday night?	_____	_____
8. Eating time and recreation time?	_____	_____

Check your schedule with the one found in Appendix B of your textbook.

Now that you have completed Activity 2.4, do a schedule for yourself. With the blank weekly schedule in the *Student Activity Book,* make your weekly schedule for next week. Place it in your notebook. At the end of one week, go back over your schedule and analyze how well you kept to your schedule. Ask yourself, did I have more time for myself because I planned this week? Did I accomplish all the work I needed to do? Was my schedule realistic?

ACTIVITY 2.5   Complete a weekly schedule for yourself on the *My Weekly Schedule* found in your *Student Activity Book* page 21.

How Can You Plan for a Longer Period of Time?

Now that you have made a daily calendar and a weekly calendar, it is time to look at one that covers at least a month. It might even be one that covers an entire grading period. On this calendar you want to schedule events that are coming up over this period of time. These might include tests, school events, personal commitments, school projects or papers, holidays, and other important dates. By doing this, you are making sure you will meet the obligations of these commitments. We call these dates *fixed commitments*. Most of us have to keep long-term calendars. People in business, industry, and government keep daily, weekly, and long-term calendars. They could not manage their time effectively without them.

ACTIVITY 2.6   Read the following set of events. Assume you are an electrical engineer and these are commitments you have to keep. Once you have read the material, fill in the monthly calendar indicating the fixed commitments.

It is the month of July. On Thursday, July 1, four things happen that affect your schedule for the month. First, a friend calls you and invites you to lunch on Tuesday, July 6th at noon. You are to meet him at the Bloody Bucket Seafood Restaurant. You accept the invitation and tell him you will meet him at 12:30. Next, your manager tells you that an important meeting has been called for the 26th at 9:00 am. You get an idea for modifying a breaker switch device and decide to spend time this month working on it at home. Your manager stops by a second time and tells you that you must write a progress report on your department and submit it to him in ten days. You also remember that you have made a commitment to help the Lions Club on the weekend of July 10th and 11th at the carnival. You are to work from 9:00 am to 1:00 pm. Finally, you have to make arrangements to attend an international conference that starts on August 5th in Dallas. You are to present a paper on your findings concerning a new electronic device to activate high powered engines. You need to prepare the report and make slides for this presentation.

Use this information and complete a monthly calendar. Turn to page 23 in your *Student Activity Booklet* and complete Activity 2.6.

ACTIVITY 2.7   Prepare your own monthly calendar on page 25 in your *Student Activity Book.*

How Much Time Should You Study?

The amount of homework due the next day as well as projects and papers due over time will determine how much time you need for study each day. Planning your study time means looking at each task and determining how long it will take you to complete each one. This is important! By projecting how much time it will take you to complete each assignment, the more likely you will concentrate on your work and get your assignments finished. *Procrastination* is the enemy of most students. Putting off what needs to be done only hurts you!

Look at the assignments you have due for tomorrow. If you have ten math problems to complete, six pages to read in your earth science book and take notes, and you need to prepare a two minute speech for language arts, how much time will you need for study that night? Before starting, write down your estimate of how long it will take you to complete the work. Complete the work. Now, check to see how accurate your predictions were on completing your assignments. Knowing your working rate will help you do a better job of planning your study time.

Another important factor in dealing with assignments is to break them down into smaller parts. For example, you were asked to prepare a two minute talk for your language arts class. In getting ready for this, you have to think about the parts of this assignment. Once you have the parts of the assignment, you can estimate the time it will take you for each part. In this case you would have to:

1. Select the topic of your speech.
2. Gather information about the topic. This might mean going to the library for your sources.
3. You will have to take notes from your sources and arrange them in logical order.
4. After this is done, you will have to practice your speech in order to memorize it. Several practices will be needed.

How much time would this take you? For some students it might take 2 or 3 hours of time. For others, it might take even more time. In any case, it is very important to look at the assignment and break it down into manageable parts. By doing this, you will see how to go about completing the task and getting it done on time!

What Is Time-on-Task?

Time-on-Task is determining how much time you will need to complete various types of assignments you get in your classes. Before beginning a study session, ask yourself the following questions:

1. How long do I estimate this assignment will take me to complete? 10, 20, 30 minutes?
2. Do I know what the assignment is asking me to do?
3. Do I have to break the task down into several manageable parts? If yes, how many?

After the study session is over, ask yourself the following questions:

1. How long did it actually take me to complete the assignment?
2. Did I concentrate and stay on the task?
3. Did I overestimate or underestimate the time I needed?
4. What about next time?

Take a clean sheet of paper and complete Exercise 2.2.

EXERCISE 2.2 Jean had the following assignments due: 15 math problems, 20 pages to read in civics and notes to take from the chapter. She estimated 25 minutes for the math and 35 minutes for the reading with 15 minutes for the notetaking. She included two breaks of five minutes each. The math took her 20 minutes, the civics an hour and 15 minutes. Why did this happen? List some reasons.

Check your reasons with those found on page 132 in Appendix B.

Even though Jean spent more time on one assignment and less on the other assignment, she planned her study session. The more planning you do, the more accurate you will get in determining the amount of time needed to complete your homework assignments.

What Happens When You Set Your Time to Study?

If you set limits for the time you intend to study each time you begin an assignment, you should see two interesting outcomes:

1. Study time will gradually decrease (more efficient time equals less study time).
2. More information will be stored in long-term memory because of the higher level of concentration taking place.

After going through these steps, there have to be some obvious rewards. We believe your grades will improve and your study time will be reduced. Last minute cramming will no longer be part of the night before the exam. You will have less pretest anxiety. You will have more free time. But the hidden payoffs are that you will break old, ineffective study habits and form new ones. Becoming more efficient and organized will be of great benefit to you in the future.

Summary

You are more likely to succeed in school if you manage your time. To manage your time effectively, keep track of important upcoming events and make commitments to study at definite times. Developing daily, weekly, monthly calendars will help you take the chance out of your life. Planning is the key to success.

Now that you have completed this chapter, take a few minutes to check yourself on the material covered. Complete the checklist found on page 27 in your *Student Activity Booklet*. (Activity 2.8)

Chapter 3
Reading for Understanding

Much of your success as a student depends heavily on your ability to read for understanding. Every author has an idea or message to get across to the reader. That message or idea is easily discovered if you can identify the *topic, main ideas,* and *details* of a passage, a chapter, or an entire book. In this book, the *topic* is study skills. The *main ideas* would be what study skills are covered in the book. The *details* would include the steps of how to do such skills as notetaking or mapping a textbook chapter.

The key to reading for understanding is being able to identify the message or idea the writer is trying to make. Your ability to answer the following questions about material you read will greatly improve your understanding of the material.

1. What is the *topic?*
2. What are the *main ideas?*
3. What *details* does the author provide to help me understand the main ideas?

What is your SSQ on Reading for Understanding? To find out your SSQ turn to page 29 in your *Student Activity Booklet* and complete the checklist. (Activity 3.0)

How Do You Find the Topic?

The topic of a passage can be found by answering the questions, "What is this *entire* passage about?" or "What does most of this passage refer to?" The answer to these questions will be the topic and will usually be one or two words. For example, as mentioned earlier, the topic of this book is "study skills."

It is important that you read the material before you try to answer the questions about the topic. Many authors will provide information about the topic in the titles of books, chapters or selections. However, you must be careful because this is not always the case. Authors may use catchy titles that arouse the curiosity of the reader but really do not help the reader identify the topic.

For example, look at the following title from a section in a science textbook:

"Looking at the Light Side"

What might this selection be about? What is the topic of this selection? Is it "a" or "b" or "c"?

a. sowbugs
b. movement of Earth about the sun
c. humor in science

Now read the selection:

Looking at the Light Side

Some investigators have found that, if sowbugs have one eye blinded and are placed between two lights, interesting results occur.* For instance, if two lamps are placed about eight inches apart and the right eye of the sowbug is covered with masking tape, the bug will circle about in a clockwise path. If the tape is placed over the left eye, the sowbug moves counterclockwise. The reason for these results is that sowbugs go to the dark. They move toward the eye that receives no light. Do you think grasshoppers and crickets would give the same reaction?

Did you answer the question about the topic correctly? You should have answered "a. sowbugs." As you can see, it is important to read titles, but don't rely on them to tell you the topic of the material to be read. Read the material first, then identify the topic.

How Can You Locate the Main Ideas?

If you are having difficulty identifying the main idea of paragraphs or long selections, chances are you also have trouble understanding what you read.

Many readers confuse main ideas with the topic. Main ideas can be found by asking, "What is the author saying about the topic?" The following steps will help you become more efficient in finding main ideas:

1. Look for the topic.
   Read the passage. Ask yourself, "What is this entire passage about?"
2. Find the main idea(s).
   Go back and examine the passage. Is there any information that is repeated or emphasized throughout the passage? Does the author appear to make any statements about the topic? What stands out as being very important? Is it very likely that your answers to these questions will be main ideas for the passage you are reading?

Main ideas can usually be stated in sentence form. For example, some of the main ideas you have come across in your reading of this text would include:

—It is important to set learning goals for myself.
—Wise planning of my time will help me become a successful student.

Read the following passage:

The most common myth about alligators is that they use their tails as weapons. The alligator is armed with powerful jaws. As he attacks his prey, his long tail simply aids him as he changes position. His tail is used not for defense, but for balance. Another popular myth is that alligators bask in the sun. Yet, alligators cannot stand very hot or very cold temperatures. In fact, strong sunlight will cause them to burn, blister, and peel. To escape heat or cold, they head for the nearest water. Many myths surround the alligator, but few of them have any basis in fact.

What is this passage about? Did you say "alligators" or myths about alligators"? Both are correct. This is the topic of the passage. What is the author saying about alligators? The author tells us that there are many myths surrounding the alligator. Since this is what the rest of the passage is about, this is the main idea. This is what the author is trying to tell you. If you were to write the main idea in your own words, you might write something like this: The main idea of this passage is: "there are some beliefs about alligators that really are not true."
Turn to page 31 in your *Student Activity Booklet* and complete Activity 3.1.

Biological Sciences Curriculum Study. The Colorado College, Colorado Springs, CO 80903

How Do You Identify Details?

Much of your reading requires you to identify and remember details related to main ideas. These are often referred to as details because the author uses them to support and clarify the main idea.

For example, look at the following paragraph:

> The automobile is the primary means of transportation in this country. Approximately 70% of the households own motor vehicles. Of these, about 60% own passenger cars. Forty percent of American households own two or more vehicles. Sixty percent own passenger cars and 25% own pickup trucks. A quickly growing interest among Americans is recreational vehicles. Fifteen percent of the households now own these vehicles.

The topic of this paragraph is *automobiles*. The main idea of the paragraph is that automobiles are the number one means of transportation in the United States. To find the details the author uses to support and clarify the main idea, you might ask, "What information does the author give to support the main idea?" "How do we know this to be true?" In the case of this paragraph, the author provides statistics to show why the automobile is the number one means of transportation. The author gives the following statistics:

—70% of households in the U.S. own motor vehicles.
—60% of these own one vehicle.
—40% own 2 or more vehicles.
—60% own passenger cars.
—25% own pickups.
—15% own recreational vehicles.

Turn to page 33 in your *Student Activity Booklet* and complete Activity 3.2.

How Do You Find the Topic, Main Ideas, and Details of Longer Selections?

You will increase your understanding of material you read or listen to if you can identify the topic, main ideas, and the details. So far we have just looked at paragraphs. The process is the same with longer passages, such as chapters, subsections, or entire books. Read the following chapter subsection.

A Horse of a Different Color

Sea horses first became known long ago because of their use as medicines.* Some people thought they could be used to cure baldness or pains in the side. Other people thought that if a live sea horse were dipped in oil of roses it would drive away fever and chills. Some people even used sea horses in a love potion. Well, we don't use sea horses this way anymore. However, they are still unusual fish to see and read about, even though most people don't normally think of them as fish. They have gills for breathing, a dorsal fin on the back, and small fins on the front. These fins move the sea horse through the water, and at full speed they beat 35 times each second. To change direction, the sea horse jerks its head to change its balance much like a diver might do in performing a complicated dive off a springboard. If the sea horse doesn't want to move, it can wrap its tail around a piece of seaweed and stay there.

Although the sea horse can move its fins rapidly, it really cannot swim very fast. So to catch the live food that it eats, the sea horse has developed a mouth that has jet-like suction and pinpoint accuracy. If a young brine shrimp swims within one and one-half inches of the sea horse's mouth, it is sucked into the mouth so quickly that you cannot even see it happen. One sea horse can eat as many as 3600 brine shrimp in a day.

Biological Sciences Curriculum Study. The Colorado College, Colorado Springs, CO 80903

One of the strangest things about sea horses is that the male sea horse carries the eggs in a kangaroo-like pouch until they hatch. To get the eggs into the pouch, the male and female go through a special way of courting behavior. They "hold tails" while the male bows to the female repeatedly. As he bows, he pumps his pouch full of water. Then he empties the water through a tiny hole in the pouch and the female lays the eggs into this hole. The eggs develop in this pouch, and in eight to ten days, the live sea horses come out of the tiny hole, one by one.

Many magazines advertise live sea horses for sale. They can be difficult to keep alive, but maybe you would like to try. They could be a lot of fun to study.

Turn to page 35 in your *Student Activity Booklet* and complete Activity 3.3.

More Practice

When you are reading longer passages for understanding, it is helpful to look at the way the author has put the passage together. Most authors state the main ideas at the beginning of the passage. Later they will restate them throughout the rest of the passage, as well as in the summary. Read the following passage and watch for the ideas that are repeated. On a separate sheet of paper, list the main ideas and at least two details for each main idea.

*Transportation**

Transportation is the movement of people and goods from place to place. It is the key to our economic system of buying and selling products. All of the things we use, eat, and wear comes to us by truck, train, ship, or plane. To move these goods there must be lines of transportation. This is why we have so many highways, railroads, sky and water lanes. These lanes cover the whole earth today.

We must be able to move goods to the places where they are needed and wanted. We also must be able to get the people to places where there are jobs and education. The most important means of transporting goods today are by trucks, trains, airplanes, and boats.

Each year more and more trucks can be found on the highways. As many as half of the cities in our country depend on trucks to deliver food and other goods. Railroads and trucks have competed with each other for business for many years. In recent times, they have begun to work together. One way they do this is by hauling freight by piggyback. Truck trailers are loaded and placed on railroad cars. The train takes these to a certain point. Then they are hooked to a truck and driven directly to a factory or warehouse.

Travel by boat was one of the very first ways man used to move goods from place to place. This type of travel is slow but large and heavy loads can be carried cheaply. Today freight moves along the rivers by large barges. The Mississippi River and the rivers that flow into it make up our largest inland system. Great ships can carry large amounts of cargo on the sea. Most products sent to other nations are moved by ship.

In the last few years one of the most important kinds of transportation has been the ship that carries oil from place to place. These ships are called "tankers." The size of these ships is larger than any other type of ship. Some can carry more than 300,000 tons of oil.

Travel by air is the newest form of transportation to develop. In the 1970's a Boeing 747 jet was built that can carry almost 500 people or 100 tons of freight. Goods carried by air can reach any point in the world within only a few hours. The cost of this kind of travel has become more reasonable in the last few years and will probably be used more and more in the future.

*Taken from *Content Inventories*, Kendall/Hunt Publishing Co., 1979.

Did you list the following as main ideas?

a) movement of goods and people
b) different forms of transportation

These are the two major ideas (main ideas) in this passage. For each of these main ideas, you could have listed a number of details. For example:

a) movement of goods and people

—key to economic system
—need good lines of transportation
—to where they are needed and wanted
—to jobs and education

b) different forms of transportation

—trucks deliver ½ food, etc. to cities
—trucks/R.R. working together
—ships carry large loads
—planes are the fastest way

This is the process you should follow when you read for understanding. It can also be applied to information presented in class lectures.

The next chapter will discuss the PREP Study System that will help you become a more active reader and learner.

Summary

As you read a textbook or listen to a class discussion it is important to be able to identify the main idea(s) as well as the details. Your job as a student is to discover which ideas are the important ones, to find them, and to understand them. The ability to read for understanding and to find main ideas and details is the base for developing good reading/study skills.

Now that you have completed this chapter, take a few minutes to check yourself on the material covered. Complete the checklist found on page 37 in your *Student Activity Booklet*.

Chapter 4
Flexible Reading and the PREP Study System

Flexible reading can be compared to shifting the gears of a car. Many of today's cars have a five speed transmission or gear box. Each gear has a specific purpose. The driver chooses the gear while driving that will make the car run effectively and efficiently. The same is true for the flexible reader. It is necessary for the reader to adjust the reading rate to fit each reading situation. There are three main factors that determine how fast you can effectively read: 1) the difficulty of the material; 2) your reading purpose; and 3) the writer's purpose. The goal is for you to understand each of these before you start to read any material.

What is your SSQ on Flexible Reading and the PREP Study System? To find out your SSQ turn to page 39 in your *Student Activity Booklet* and complete the checklist.

What Does It Mean to be a Flexible Reader?

A flexible reader is one who realizes and understands that all materials are not read at the same rate. Some materials are more difficult than others—a comic book is easier to read than a math textbook. A magazine reads differently than a novel. A story may be easier to read and understand than a science textbook. Each reading task has a different purpose and should be handled accordingly. A flexible reader will adjust and choose the reading rate and purpose to fit the material.

How Do You Become a Flexible Reader?

To become a flexible reader you need to ask yourself the following:

1. *What's my purpose in reading?* You need to ask yourself the following questions:
    Am I reading this material for fun, enjoyment, or learning?
    Do I want to put the material into long-term memory?
    What is my purpose for reading this material?
    What do I want to get out of this reading?
2. *Why did the teacher assign the material?* Do I need to read for the details or to be ready to answer questions in class? Will I be asked to discuss the ideas in class? Am I preparing for a test? Depending on the answer(s), you will decide how to read the assignment.
3. *What is the purpose of the author?* Does the author want to inform, entertain, persuade, discuss alternatives, raise questions, or just have you read for enjoyment? It is important for you to determine what messages the author is sending to the reader. In this way, you will be better able to read the material. In the material that follows, we will show you how to use the PREP Study System as a way of becoming a flexible, effective reader.

What Is the PREP Study System?

PREP is an acronym for a reading/study system that will help you become an active reader.* It will also help you understand what you are reading and remember it longer. The PREP system has four major parts:

1. PREVIEWING is getting an overview of the material through reading the introductory paragraph, the concluding or summary paragraph, and by looking at headings and subheadings for an overall organization of the chapter.
2. READING ACTIVELY means becoming totally involved with the material, taking notes, mapping, and asking yourself questions about the material as you read. An active reader is one who asks a lot of questions.
3. EXAMINING forces you to become involved with the material by asking and answering questions once you have gotten your notes. It is at this point that you develop questions about the material.
4. PROMPTING is using memory skills and techniques to help you recall the material. One of the most effective ways of remembering is through verbal recitation. Another is asking questions and answering them. The goal of prompting is to help you get new information into long-term memory.

Why Use the PREP System?

A system like PREP is necessary because study-type reading is more demanding than pleasure reading. Becoming an effective reader in school by using a system like PREP will help you:

a) learn more.
b) understand more fully what you are reading.
c) put information into long-term memory.
d) become a more productive student.

When Should You Use the PREP System?

The PREP System can be used in *all* areas of reading but especially in the content areas (science, social studies, English, mathematics). The reader can choose whether to use all four steps of PREP or individual steps. The steps used will usually depend on the material being read. The chart below gives some examples of how the PREP System can be used in reading different materials.

Applying PREP to Different Reading Situations

	Preview	Read	Examine	Prompt
Newspaper		X		
Book for a Report	X	X	X	X
Textbook	X	X	X	X
Poem	X	X	X	
Directions on a model		X		
Magazines for reports	X	X	X	
Books for Entertainment		X		

*Reprinted with permission of Twin Oaks Publishing, Inc.

Why Preview Material?

Previewing material helps you get ready to read actively and serves these purposes for most reading situations:

1. It helps serve as a warmup for later, more careful reading.
2. It helps you ask these questions: What do I think the story will be about? What do I already know about this topic? What do I want to know?
3. It helps increase your reading rate.
4. It helps you increase your understanding of the material.
5. It gives you an overview of what the material is about.

Also, recalling information you know about the topic will help promote concentration. Associating new information with previous ideas is a major learning technique.

There is one more advantage to previewing. It gets you actively involved, and it helps reduce mind-wandering and daydreaming which happens to many students as they study.

What Are the Steps in Previewing?

There are five steps you should use when previewing new material. The steps are:

1. Read the title and take some time to think about it.
2. Examine all pictures, graphs, charts, and other visual aids.
3. Read introduction and/or opening paragraph.
4. Read closing paragraph or summary and the questions at the end of the material.
5. Determine organization of the chapters by looking at bold headings and subheadings.

Now look at each step in more detail.

Step 1: *Read the title.*

The title usually announces the topic to the reader. When you preview, you should call to mind what you already know about the topic from past experience. Then, ask yourself these questions:

What do I think the material will be about?
What do I already know about the topic?
What do I want to know about the topic?

Turn to page 41 in your *Student Activity Booklet* and complete Activities 4.1 and 4.2.

Step 2: *Look at pictures, graphs, or illustrations.*

People have said "a good picture is worth a thousand words." This is particularly true in previewing. A graph, chart, or picture, can tell you a great deal about the material as well as clarify ideas and give direction to your thinking. Often the illustration in a textbook shows a complex idea in "picture" form which is easier for you to understand. So, don't pass up the illustrations in your reading. Take time to look at them, read what they say, and use them to learn the new information.

Turn to page 45 in your *Student Activity Booklet* and complete Activity 4.3.

Step 3: *Read the introduction or opening paragraphs.*

This section is the author's first chance to communicate with the reader. Most authors will use this opening paragraph to give you some information about the background of the chapter or article. It is at this point the author gives you an idea of what the material will be about.

Step 4: *Read the closing paragraph or summary.*

Go to the end of the selection and read the last paragraph or summary. This helps pull together the main ideas in the selection. The author will usually summarize the important facts for you. Reading the first and last paragraphs will help you understand what the author feels is important. If there are questions at the end of the selection, read those over before you actively read. The questions give you clues to the important information in the selection.

Turn to page 47 in your *Student Activity Booklet* and complete Activities 4.4 and 4.5.

Step 5: *Use the headings and subheadings for organization of the material.*

The last step of the preview step is to look over the material quickly and locate the headings and subheadings. By using this, the reader may discover the author's organization of the selection. For example, you may find in a textbook chapter that the presentation is divided into three main topics with three subheadings for each main topic. This will tell you to pay close attention to the three main topics to be presented. Therefore, as you preview, you should note the organization used by the author before you actively read the material.

Next, turn to page 51 in your *Student Activity Booklet* and complete Activity 4.6.

How Can You Become Actively Involved When You Read?

This happens when you become totally involved with the material. The way you approach the different types of reading tasks will depend on the content of the material as well as your purpose for reading. In courses like geography, science, civics, home economics, math, or language arts, you need to become actively involved with the material. By doing this, you are more likely to recall the important information later. You begin with the preview step where you get an overview of the content as well as the general organization of the selection. Next, you begin to actively read the material in detail. Several reading/study techniques are available to you during the active reading time. They include:

1. Finding the main ideas(s) of the material and supporting details.
2. Taking notes for later study.
3. Writing summary statements.
4. Mapping the material.

Finding the Main Idea

In Chapter 3 of this book we discussed finding the main idea. Take a few minutes to review this chapter and get yourself ready to become an active reader.

Taking Notes for Later Use

Taking notes has three main purposes: (1) it helps you get actively involved with the material, (2) it helps you get the main points of the selection into your own words, and (3) it helps you later when you go back to study the information in detail. By taking good notes you will not have to reread the material. This is a goal you want to reach. More information about notetaking will be presented in Chapter 5.

Writing Summary Statements

By writing a summary statement about the material you have read, you are condensing the important information into a few sentences. Like an author of a textbook or an article, you are reducing the most important points into a summary paragraph. This will be useful to you later as you review the material for tests. More will be said about the summary statement in Chapter 5.

Mapping Information

Mapping is notes in "picture" form. Instead of taking regular notes you would arrange information into a picture representing the information. By doing this you would have a graphic representation of the information presented in the material. The following map shows the PR steps of the PREP Study System we just covered in this chapter. Mapping will be covered in more detail in Chapter 6.

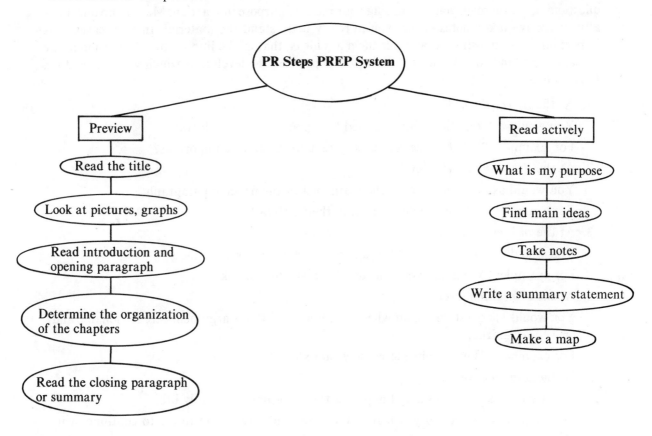

Summary

An English teacher once gave this comment to the class while reading a story: "If you want to understand a book, you must live it. You must feel the rain on your face, the warmth from the sun, the joy, sadness, and frustrations described in the story." In short, you want to become a part of what you are reading rather than just reading words. How much you become involved in the material depends on your *interest, purpose in reading, and willingness to become involved.*

Why Is Examining an Important Part of PREP?

Examining and active reading go hand in hand. As you are reading you are *examining* the material for main ideas and important information. One way to do this is to ask yourself questions. Based on your purpose(s), the type of questions will vary. In any event, a characteristic of a good reader is one who can ask questions while reading.

Why Ask Teacher-like Questions?

Books are a store-house of information. What you want to be able to do is get that information from the material to long-term memory. In order to understand the material you often need to ask questions. Try to ask "teacher-type" questions whenever possible. These will help you "think" about the material you are trying to learn. By becoming actively involved in developing questions about the material, you can usually answer your own questions.

When Should You Ask Yourself Questions about the Material?

Questions can be made up while reading the material or after you have taken notes. By questioning as you read, you are turning your reading purpose into action. Making up questions after you have taken notes causes you to really understand the material. In both cases, it is important to ask questions that cover the main ideas, that is, the important information in the passage. The kinds of questions you ask will depend on the level(s) at which you are reading. For example:

1. At the *literal detail* level:

   You would ask questions that are used to support the main idea(s).

   For Example: "What is one reason why regular exercise is important?"

2. At the *literal main-idea* level:

   You would ask questions about the main idea of the passage paragraph.

   For example: "Why do eagles remain in their habitat?"

3. At the *inferential* level:

   You would ask questions about a judgment made from known facts.

   For example: "What can you conclude from smelling smoke?"

4. At the *evaluation* level:

   You would ask questions about whether or not the author's arguments are reasonable and/ or well-organized.

   For example: "How convincing is the writer's point?"

5. At the *applied* level

   You would ask questions about applying this information in daily life.

   For example: "What did you learn that would encourage you to try to continue swimming?"

Questions force you to give answers. Answers require action on your part. When making up good teacher-like questions on the material you are reading, you are causing yourself to learn!

How Do You Get Started Writing Questions?

One easy way to come up with *literal-level* questions when reading is to change headings and subheadings into questions using the words "how," "when," "what," "where," "why," and "who." By doing this you are more likely to remember the answers to your questions. Also, headings and subheadings are useful to help you make questions to be used in the *recall column* of your notes. Another way of writing questions is to use the summary statement in a chapter. Simply change each sentence in the summary to a question.

More will be covered about this topic in Chapter 5.

How Can You Improve Your Memory?

The purpose of the prompting step is to develop ways to remember the material. A good memory is important in school and later in your career. In school you want to place as much information into long-term memory as possible. Later, you want to be able to use that information in almost every part of your life. Developing good memory skills is important.

What Are Some Ways That You Can Use to Remember New Material?

There are several things you can do to help you remember material you want to learn and retain. YOU CAN:

1. Have a *DESIRE* to *remember* the material. Concentrate while you read and study.
2. Look for ways to *apply* what you are learning in your daily life. Ask yourself, "How can I use this information?"
3. Make a *list of questions* over the material and *answer them.*
4. *Recite* what you are trying to learn. This self-testing technique is one of the most powerful memory aids.
5. *Explain* the new information to a friend. If you can talk about it, you know it.
6. *Discuss* the *main ideas* and other important points in a group discussion.
7. *Superlearn* the material. *Drill* until the information is part of you.
8. *Space your learning sessions.* Don't wait until the last minute to study. Space a number of short sessions over a period of time. Avoid the last minute rush!
9. *Organize the information* you want to learn into groups. Learning theorists indicate you should not have more than *seven* groups about one topic. Once you have your groups, place the details you are working with under each heading. Chapter headings and subheadings can often be used as the groups. Use these whenever possible. More on this will be covered in Chapter 6.

Why Is It So Easy to Forget What You Have Read?

The "interference theory" may help you understand why you forget much of what you have just read. It says that new information wipes out old information. Even though you understand the old, when you read the new, the new sometimes takes over the old. The same thing can happen when you are listening to a lecture or class discussion. Even though you understand what you hear or read at that moment, you may not be able to retain it because your attention switches to something else. To avoid this, you must learn how to take good notes.

Why Write a Summary Statement?

In this activity you identify the main topics and ideas and restate them in your own words as much as possible. You are pulling together the main points the writer presented in the chapter, article, or passage. By doing this, you are thinking about the entire passage and are forced to tie it together. In just a few sentences you write a summary of the material you are trying to learn.

How Do You Write a Summary?

It requires an understanding of the main ideas of the passage and the ability to write these thoughts. Use these guidelines to help you:

1. Keep the *order* of the passage. Summarize from the beginning of the passage to the end of the passage.
2. Keep the important ideas. Eliminate the details of the passage.
3. Write the summary in your *own* words as much as possible. Be concise.
4. Be sure to get the most important ideas in your summary.

Writing summaries every time you complete a set of notes, finish reading a chapter or article, or complete a discussion about new information is a must!

EXERCISE 4.1 Now that we have gone through all the steps of the PREP Study System, it is now time to practice. Read the article "Flying Seeds." Use the various parts of the PREP Study System while reading this article. On a sheet of paper, do the following:

First, PREVIEW the article. Answer these questions:

1. What does the title of the article tell me about the topic?

2. What do the headings and subheadings tell me about the organization and the meaning of the material?

3. What information did I get from the opening paragraph and the ending paragraph?

Second, ACTIVELY READ the article. Answer these questions:

1. What is the topic of the article?

2. What are the main ideas that were presented?

3. What information do I need in my notes to help me remember the material?

Third, Write one QUESTION for each of the five types of questions pointed out under *examine* (see p. 236):

1. *Literal detail:*

2. *Literal main-idea:*

3. *Inferential:*

4. *Evaluation:*

5. *Applied:*

Finally, use some PROMPTING techniques to learn this material. Which ones did you use?

Traveling Seeds
by Cheryl Morgan

Flying

Most traveling seeds go by air.* When you blow off a dandelion's fluffy white head, you are doing just what the wind does—spreading its seeds. Dandelion and milkweed seeds are attached to silky parachutes that help carry them through the air. Cottonwood seeds are covered with fine hairs that help them fly through the air.

Maple, elm, and many pine seeds are like little helicopters. They have wings that whirl in the wind, carrying them far from the parent trees.

There are seeds so small and light they need no parachutes, hairs, or wings to help them fly. People in airplanes have collected grass seeds 915 meters (3000 feet) in the air! Orchid seeds are as fine as dust. Just one ripe orchid pod holds millions. If you breathe on them gently, they billow up like a cloud. The wind can blow tiny seeds like these for hundreds of kilometers.

Other seeds use the wind to travel along the ground. Some seeds fall after the first snow, and the wind sends them sledding over the frozen surface. When the snow melts, they may sink down to the earth and start to grow.

Other seeds cartwheel across the ground. Have you ever seen big, brown tumbleweeds blowing across a desert or prairie? When these bushes are full of ripe seeds, they dry out and the root shrivels up. Then the first wind to come along uproots the plant and rolls it along the ground, scattering seeds as it goes.

Floating

A few plants send their seeds for river or ocean cruises. Some plants that grow in the water release their seeds there. The American lotus—a kind of water lily—does this. Its seed pod is a sturdy little boat that can float for a long time.

Other plants grow along the water's edge. Their seeds fall in and drift downstream. If you look closely along a stream bank, you can often see clusters of sprouted seeds that have floated to shore.

Coconut trees have sailing seeds too. The trees grow in large groves along tropical beaches, and many coconuts fall into the ocean. Because the nut is waterproof and floats, the seed inside stays dry in its own "life jacket." Usually it just bobs along the coast until it is tossed onto shore to root and grow. But sometimes a coconut drifts out to sea and floats on the ocean's currents to a distant island.

Exploding

Can you imagine plants that snap, crackle, and pop? Tap the touch-me-not's seed pod and it explodes with a snap! The pod is made of five little strips that grow tighter and tighter over the seeds inside. When ripe, the strips spring apart at the slightest touch. They hit the seeds and flip them in all directions.

The seed pod of the wild geranium is spring-loaded too. But its seeds are attached to the springs. When the springs snap, they throw out the seeds the way you throw a baseball.

Have you ever pinched a slippery watermelon seed between your thumb and finger and poppped it away? This is how violet and witch hazel plants scatter their seeds. The sides of the seed pods open at one end and squeeze harder and harder on the seeds inside. Pinch. POP!

Hitchhiking

Some seeds hitchhike. The next time your dog bites at a sticker in his fur, look for the hooks or claws the seed uses to hitch a ride. Cockleburs, burdocks, and sticktights all travel like this. They are bitten, brushed, or bumped off somewhere along the way, to begin another pesky plant.

There are some seeds that will hitch rides on the muddy feet of swamp creatures. A migrating duck with dirty feet can carry seeds hundreds of kilometers away.

Some seeds have a sticky coat that helps them hitchhike. Oily mistletoe seeds stick to birds' beaks. At clean-up time, the birds wipe their bills on tree branches, leaving the mistletoe seeds behind.

Animals can be helpful litterbugs. When squirrels hide walnuts and hickory nuts for a winter's snack, some may be forgotten and begin to grow. The chickaree, a little red squirrel, opens sequoia cones to eat the seeds inside. As he nibbles away he scatters some of the seeds around. Blue jays dig holes with their bills and bury acorns. But just like the squirrels, they often forget to come back for the food.

Even animals who swallow seeds help them to travel. Some seeds are digested, but many—like the raspberry, cherry, and saguaro—pass undigested through the animals' bodies to sprout and grow.

Birds sometimes plant trees this way. In the eastern United States, you can see red cedar trees stretched out in long straight rows. Perhaps years ago a fence was there, and cedar waxwings came to perch and eat their favorite food—the fruit of the red cedar. The undigested seeds of their dinners grew into a long line of trees that kept growing long after the fence had rotted away.

You help seeds travel too—when you pop a touch-me-not pod or when cockleburs stick to your socks. And where did you spit out last summer's watermelon seeds?

Check your answers with those listed in Appendix B.

Summary

One of the goals in reading is not to see how many books you get through but how many books get into you. This is where the PREP Reading/Study System can help you. It can be used or adapted to fit any reading situation. PREP gives you an organized approach to reading/ studying as well as specific skills and techniques to become a better reader and student.

Nothing takes the place of effort, determination, and a willingness to work in order to become a good student. But the application of *PREP* and *hard work* will increase your productivity and help you become a more successful student.

Now that you have completed this chapter, take a few minutes to check yourself on the material covered. Complete the checklist found on page 53 in your *Student Activity Booklet*. (Activity 4.7)

Chapter 5
Notetaking

Notetaking is primarily a means of recording information for later use. As we mentioned in the Active Reading part of the PREP Study System, notetaking is one way to become an active reader. Students usually have some sort of a notetaking system. In this chapter, we will show you a way to take effective notes. The Summary Sheet System consists of three parts: (1) your notes; (2) recall column questions; and (3) a summary. The parts of this notetaking system will be discussed in more detail later.

What is your SSQ on notetaking? To find out your SSQ turn to page 55 in your *Student Activity Booklet* and complete the checklist under Activity 5.0.

When Do You Take Notes?

Notes are taken when you want to keep a record of what is happening. This information can later be used to review for tests or just to learn. Notetaking is used while listening to *lectures* or when taking notes from *textbooks* and other written material.

Where Do You Take Notes?

People have taken notes on napkins, envelopes, notebooks, and textbooks. Notebooks come in all sizes. The smaller notebook is easier to carry, but notes are usually cramped on the page and more difficult to read. Two excellent ways to keep notes are in a *spiral notebook* or in a *three-ring loose-leaf notebook*. If you use a spiral notebook, have one for each class. The spiral notebooks are easy to carry. When writing in a spiral notebook, write only on the right-hand sheet. This will allow additional notes to be added on the left hand sheet if necessary.

The other possibility is a three-ring loose-leaf notebook. This is the most flexible notebook. Pages can be added or taken out easily. All class notes from lectures and printed material can be in the same place. Whichever one you choose, it is important to have a *specific place* to keep your notes. Always date your notes.

Is Listening a Part of Notetaking?

An important part of taking notes is *active listening*. As a notetaker you must listen for the main ideas of the lecture as well as the details. Your job is to record *this information* in your notebook.

What Is Active Listening?

Active listening is becoming involved with what is happening around you. To become a more active listener you need to:

1. *Stop talking.* You cannot listen if you are talking.
2. *Have a desire to listen*—concentrate on what the speaker is saying. Don't let your mind wander or your personal feelings get in the way.
3. *Sit close to the speaker.* It has been shown through research that listening improves when you are at the front of the room.
4. *Remove distractions.* Don't doodle, tap, or shuffle papers. Outside distractions get in the way of listening.
5. *Listen for main ideas.* Good listeners concentrate on the main ideas rather than facts, dates, names. Ask yourself questions: "What is the speaker really saying to me," and "in what way do the details support the main ideas?"
6. *Ask questions.* This will show the teacher that you are listening. By asking good questions, you will cause yourself to be "tuned in" to the discussion.

Should You Take Notes in Outline Form?

One form of notetaking is the outline system. This notetaking system has been used for many years. The outline form has a series of main categories under which is grouped related, more specific information. The system looks like this:

1. Topic
   A. First Main Idea
      1. First detail
      2. Second detail
   B. Second Main Idea
      1. First detail
      2. Second detail

There are disadvantages to this system. Most teachers do not present information in a form that can be organized and outlined in this manner. Students usually become confused about whether to use A, B, 1, or 2. This is a problem and could prevent you from taking good notes.

An alternative to the outline method is the Summary Sheet System on notetaking.* This system begins by dividing the paper into two columns: (1) the *Recall Column* and (2) the *Notetaking Column.* Look at EXAMPLE 5.1. Notice that the recall column is 2½ inches in

*Reprinted with permission of Twin Oaks Publishing, Inc.

width. You will have to draw a line on notebook paper to make this column. The page looks like this:

EXAMPLE 5.1

Recall Column (2½″)	Note Column (6″)
	Topic
	Main Idea
	Details
	Details
	Main Idea
	Details
	Details
	Summary

How Do You Take Notes Using the Summary Sheet System?

The notes are recorded as fully and as meaningfully as possible. The notes are recorded on the right side of the six inch space. *Abbreviations* should be used whenever possible. When using this system, numbers or letters are not usually necessary unless the speaker gives you those specific clues. It is helpful to you to categorize information by indenting and spacing. The (1) *topic* is written to the far left and underlined in the note column. This will help you in the overall organization of the notes. (2) Main ideas statements are indented about an inch to the right and (3) the *details* are indented to the right under the main idea statements. Look at EXAMPLE 5.2 and see the different parts of this system including the *note column, recall column,* and *summary*.

EXAMPLE 5.2

Recall Column	Note Column	
	Cell Theory (Topic)	
Why are cells important?	All organisms are made of cells.	(Main Idea)
	Cell is the basic unit of structure	
	Cell is a basic building block	Details
	Cells are too tiny to see without a microscope	
	Microscope is used to study cells	
	Microscope has many parts	(Main Idea)
Describe the different parts of a microscope.	arm	
	body tube	
	eyepiece	
	revolving eyepiece	
	high/low power objective lens	Details
	adjustment knob	
	stage and stage clips	
	diaphragm	
	mirror	
	base	
	Summary: Cells form the basic structure of all organisms. Cells are too tiny to see without a microscope. A microscope has many different parts.	

What Is the Recall Column?

The recall column is located within the 2½ inch space. The purpose of the recall column is to reduce ideas and facts to specific questions about the notes. When you finish your notes, you will write questions about your notes. This will help you remember the information. Later, as you go back to study the notes, you will use the recall questions to help you self-test yourself over the material. If you can answer the questions without looking at the notes, you have most likely learned the information.

What Is the Summary?

At the end of your notes is the summary. Writing summaries can be difficult at the beginning, but the more you practice, the better you will get at writing good summaries.

Summaries identify the purpose, as well as the main ideas. Try to restate the purpose, topics, and main ideas in your own words as much as possible. Writing the summary causes you to pull all the parts of the passage together in one short statement. If you can write a summary, you will have a good understanding of the most important ideas stated in the material.

Look at EXAMPLE 5.3. See how all the parts of the Summary Sheet System of Notetaking are used. Notice the *topic* is *Killer Smoke*. Under this are four *main ideas* including: (1) cause of death in fires, (2) how to control smoke, (3) cost of smoke control, and (4) benefits of smoke control. Under each main idea you will find a number of *details* which help you remember the important points the author is presenting.

EXAMPLE 5.3

Recall Column	Note Column
What is the major cause of death in fire?	*Killer Smoke (Topic)* 　*Cause of death in fires* (Main Idea) 　　80% of people who die in fires die of smoke, not fire 　　—e.g. MGM fire, Las Vegas, 1980, 84 killed, only 12 from fire 　　—smoke produces toxic clouds: carbon monoxide, fumes from plastic
	How to control smoke (Main Idea)
What are 2 ways to control smoke?	2 main ways: 　　　1. Vent smoke out, air conditioning left on, blow smoke out
Explain "pressurize."	2. Pressurize air, fire can be localized with air pressure 　　Many buildings beginning to smoke proof 　　May become "code" in many cities
What is the cost of smoke control?	*Cost of smoke control* (Main Idea) 　　not high considering alternative 　　adds $1 per sq. ft. to building cost 　　lowers insurance costs
What is the most important benefit of smoke control?	*Benefits of smoke control* (Main Idea) 　　save lives 　　reduce lawsuits in case of fire 　　helps firemen get rid of long-term problems with smoke inhalation
	Summary—Smoke kills more people than the actual fire. There are effective and fairly inexpensive ways of smoke proofing buildings that will help to save both property and lives.

Now read the following passage. Look at Example 5.4 of the notes taken from this passage. Do they represent the important ideas? Do the notes have enough detail?

Left-Handers Unite!

"The only thing I can do with my right hand is scratch my left elbow!"* Sandy recently broke her left wrist. She said, "At least the break will not interfere with your school work." Sandy's comment reminded him that she is left-handed.

Sandy is one of a minority group of people who do most common tasks with their left hands. For many years, educators felt it was important for everyone to write with their right hand. But left-handers insisted on using their left hands. It felt more natural.

*Charles H. Heinler, FOCUS ON LIFE SCIENCE. Charles E. Merrill Publishing Company, A Bell & Howell Company, Columbus, OH 43216 Copyright © 1977, 1974, 1969 by Bell & Howell.

Left-handers are more respected today. In school they are now taught to write correctly using their left hands. But all is still not easy for left-handers in a predominately right-handed world. Many items have to be especially made for left-handers. Specialty shops that carry such items as left-handed guitars, golf clubs, and can openers have opened in some cities. The Association for the Protection of the Rights of Left-Handers promotes the manufacture and sale of items for left-handers. It also educates right-handers about the problems left-handers face.

Although many studies have been made and much research has been done, no one knows why some people prefer to use their left hand instead of their right. Scientists have suggested that left-handedness may be an inherited behavior. Others believe that it is acquired. Still other researchers think that left-handers' brains may function differently than the brains of right-handers. Much more study is needed to determine the cause of left-handedness. If you are a left-hander, you are not alone. Many famous people such as Ben Franklin, Leonardo da Vinci, Queen Victoria, Pablo Picasso, and Babe Ruth were left-handers, too!

EXAMPLE 5.4

Recall Column	Notes
	Left-Handers Unite (Topic)
Why do left-handers feel better today?	*World is mainly a right-handed world* (Main Idea) Left-handers are more respected today easier for left-handers to obtain left-handed items (golf clubs, guitars, can openers)
What does the APRLH promote?	*Association for the Protection of the Rights of Left-Handers* (Main Idea) encourages and promotes left-handed items. No one knows why people prefer left hand over right
What does research say about why one is left-handed?	*Research:* has suggested left-handedness is inherited behavior (Main Idea) left-handedness could be an acquired trait left-handers brain functions differently than right-handers
What famous people were left-handed?	*People* (Main Idea) Famous people are left-handed: examples—Ben Franklin, Leonardo da Vinci, Picasso, Babe Ruth, Queen Victoria.
	Summary: The article describes how left-handers are finding it easier to survive in a right-handed world. APRLH encourages manufacturers to make more left-handed items. There is no specific reason why some people prefer the left hand over the right. There are many famous people who are left handed— Franklin, da Vinci, Picasso, Queen Victoria, Ruth.

Turn to page 57 in your *Student Activity Booklet* and complete Activity 5.1.

How Can You Write Recall Column Questions?

Several ways to form questions for the recall column are: 1) change the subheadings in textbooks or articles into questions; 2) use the questions at the end of the chapter if the author provides them; and 3) write questions that use the words why, when, where, how, describe. Some examples of recall questions might be:

Why are cells important?
Describe the different parts of a microscope.
What are the major causes of death in fires?
How can firemen control smoke in a fire?
Where are cells found?
How are cells used in the human body?
When would you use a microscope?

EXERCISE 5.0 Read the following passage. On a sheet of paper, write three recall questions you think are important in helping you understand the important messages in the passage.

Mollusks and Echinoderms

What do a clam, a snail, and an octopus have in common?* Although they look very different, they all belong to the group of animals called **mollusks** (mol´esks). All of these animals have a soft body. Most mollusks also have a large, muscular **foot**. A mollusk uses this foot to move about. The heart and other body organs are crowded together above the foot. A fold of tissue called the **mantle** encloses the foot and other organs. In many mollusks, the upper surface of the mantle produces a hard shell. In this chapter you will learn about different kinds of mollusks. You will also study a group of animals that live only in the ocean. These animals are called **echinoderms** (iki´ne dermz).

SUMMARY: Mollusks are soft-bodied animals. A fold of tissue called the mantle may enclose the body organs and a muscular foot. In many mollusks, the mantle secretes a substance that forms a hard shell. Mollusks are an important source of food for humans. Echinoderms are spiny-skinned animals. Most echinoderms move about with the help of spines and special tube feet. All the echinoderms live in the ocean.

Did you have some of the following questions?

1) How would you describe a mollusk?
2) How does a mollusk move about?
3) What is the purpose of this chapter?

4) Why do echinoderms live in the ocean?
5) Why are mollusks important to humans?

EXERCISE 5.1 Read the following passage. On a sheet of paper, write two recall column questions about the topic "Aspirin."

Aspirin: More than Commercials Tell Us

Aspirin is so easy to get and it's been around for so long, most of us don't take it very seriously. It's considered to be so safe, we rarely give it a second thought. For years, aspirin has been the standard all-purpose remedy for colds, headaches, and mild fevers. And it's been one of the standard medicines to joke about. But aspirin is no joke!

Aspirin is anything but a bland and limited drug. In fact, medical experts keep uncovering new uses for aspirin. But they may be uncovering new dangers as well. The odds are, if aspirin were a new medicine, you'd probably need a prescription for it!

Compare your questions with a classmate. Are they similar?

Check your answers with those in Appendix B.

*Life Nature Library/THE SEA by Leonard Engel and the Editors of LIFE Time-Life Books, Inc., Publisher (1961) Time Inc.

EXERCISE 5.2   Try another one. This will be a longer passage. On a separate sheet of paper write at least three recall questions about this material.

The Computer Revolution Hits Home

Everybody's talking about the "computer revolution."* But in a way, the revolution is already over. Right now, computer technology could make this happen. . . .

You're arriving home very late one night. Your place seems strangely silent, dark—even dead. Of course, you remind yourself, it is late. But still, you feel something isn't right.

And no wonder—someone, probably accidentally, turned your home off! Once you realize it, no problem. You simply punch your I.D. number in the keypad alongside the door and that old familiar voice greets you—the voice of your computerized home.

Doors open automatically and lights switch on and off for you, as you pass from room to room. The heat and motion sensors of your computerized home keep track of your path.

When you go to bed, though, you switch off the light.

Still, your computerized home detects you lying there and selects a special, soothing recording for you—slow, soft music, or the sound of waves lapping against the shore, or maybe the sound of raindrops falling.

"Sleep Well" Says Home?

A wristband that you wear almost all of the time sends out your vital signs—including heart rate and breathing pattern—to the home, so the computer will know when you're finally asleep. As sleep deepens, your home will raise its temperature.

Of course, your home is programmed to pick the least expensive way to adjust its temperature. First, the computer checks the temperature outside. And it will spring the windows open—if that's all that's needed to keep you comfortable (unless of course, you've programmed your home to keep the windows locked).

You don't even have to set an alarm clock before you get in bed. There's no need to worry about what time you'll get up. You don't have to be anywhere in the morning. In fact, there are very few reasons left to venture outside at all.

No More School?

You'll study when it's convenient for you. Is history very easy? Do you need to go more slowly learning French? Relax. Your very own personal computer acts as your private "teacher,' giving you individualized instruction. You pick the subject you want to study, touch the keyboard, and the computer responds—instantaneously—with answers to your questions or more practice questions of its own.

Current news events, magazines, even entire libraries of books are stored by special data—collecting services. If you subscribe to these services, you can use your computer terminal to tap the special types of information you need and the subject areas that interest you most.

Did you change the subheadings into questions? What clues helped you write your questions? Compare your questions with several classmates.

Check your answers with those in Appendix B.

How Do You Write a Summary of What You Have Read or Heard?

Writing a summary is the best way to see if you have a complete idea about the topic or subject covered. In writing a summary, you want to tie together the most important ideas presented. These are the main ideas. Do not include details in your summary. Remember, you want to rewrite the main ideas of the lesson. So your summary should:

1. Be one fourth to one third the length of the original.
2. Be clear and easy to understand.
3. Contain all the main ideas that are in the original.
4. Not contain any ideas that are not in the original.
5. Be written in your own words as much as possible.

Look at the example that follows. Read the short passage on how desert animals survive. After you read the summary, examine it. Does it have the characteristics of a good summary?

Desert Animals

Nowhere in the world does sundown release so many animals from burrows as in a desert. Since early morning they have sought subterranean sanctuary from the burning glare. In twilight and darkness they emerge, detecting promptly the time when, through the clear air, the soil's surface has radiated to space enough of the excessive daytime heat. Their well-guarded store of water no longer is in such peril. Each can seek to supplement its energy supply, to find its favorite food.

Every desert-dwelling animal has some artful dodge whereby it can exist without liquid water from one year's end to the next. A few, like snails and frogs, wait underground not only from dawn to dusk but from one rain to the next, though the rains be a year apart. The rest depend on some special means for getting water. Most take it second hand from the storage reservoirs of plants. Others manufacture the simple essential water molecule from atoms gained in dry foods. Some subsist on smaller animals which have these special abilities.

Summary

Sundown permits desert animals to leave their burrows. Free of the extreme heat of day, they go forth seeking food. Every desert animal can live somehow for months without liquid water. A few, including snails and frogs, remain underground between rainfalls. Most get water from plants. Others manufacture water or survive on smaller animals.

Does the summary have the following characteristics?

1. It is one fourth to one third the length of the original.

2. It is clear and easy to understand.

3. It contains all the main ideas that are in the original.

4. It does not contain any ideas that are not in the original.

5. It is written in the student's own words as much as possible.

Now it is time for you to write a summary.

EXERCISE 5.3 On a separate sheet of paper read the following passage and write a summary about The Sea.

The Sea
Silver Burdett Company

Someday you may take an ocean trip.* If you do, you will see waves bigger than you ever imagined. Out at sea, where the water is often more than two miles deep, there are waves bigger than the biggest ship ever built. These waves are great rolling hills of water. Sometimes they are so huge that a whole ship may disappear from view completely in the valley between two waves.

On land, too, the sight of ocean waves breaking on the shore is sometimes almost unbelievable. In stormy weather, huge waves can pound any seacoast. But there are certain places on earth where waves are especially big. One of these is the very southern tip of South America. Here the great waves called Cape Horn rollers thunder against the shore.

These Cape Horn rollers are probably the biggest waves on earth. They are about a mile apart, and they move forward at close to 50 miles an hour. But their size is the impressive thing. They often reach a height of 80 or 90 feet. Imagine a wave nearly 10 stories high, traveling at 50 miles an hour.

To see these waves breaking on the shore is enough to take your breath away. Charles Darwin, one of the most famous scientists of all time, visited this area way back in 1833. Later he wrote in his diary: "One sight of such a coast is enough to make a landsman dream for a week about shipwreck, peril, and death."

The Orkney and Shetland Islands of northern Scotland are also famous for the waves along their coasts. Here, during the storms of winter, waves pound the shore with almost incredible force. So much spray is thrown into the air that the air seems filled with gray smoke, and it is sometimes hard to keep from getting lost. Not only that, but these great waves strike the shore with such force that it is possible to hear the noise 20 miles away.

There is a strange thing about waves. You have probably noticed it. Suppose you are standing on a beach. You look out and you see the waves coming in to shore. But if you throw a stick out into the waves, it stays more or less in the same place. The waves simply roll in to shore under it. Only after what seems a very long time will your stick finally wash up on the beach.

There is a simple reason why floating objects are not carried along by waves. Waves are not *things*—they are *movements*. In the sea, the water through which the waves travel moves hardly at all. This may seem hard to understand, but it is not. Imagine that you have spread a big bath towel on the floor and a little mouse runs under it. Think of the bath towel as the water and the mouse as the wave. You can see that, as the mouse runs, the towel does not move.

Check your summary with the one below.

Does the summary have the following characteristics?

1. It is one fourth to one third the length of the original.

2. It is clear and easy to understand.

3. It contains all the main ideas that are in the original.

4. It does not contain any ideas that are not in the original.

5. It is written in your own words as much as possible.

*Life Nature Library/THE SEA By Leonard Engel and The Editors of LIFE Time-Life Books Inc., Publishers (1961) Time Inc.

Example of Summary Statement:

Whether a person is on land or sea, waves are impressive because of their size, speed, and force. Waves can be as high as a ten story building and travel at speeds of 50 mph. The islands of northern Scotland are famous for their large waves. Waves are movements—not things. This means that the water through which the wave travels moves hardly at all, which may be hard to understand.

EXERCISE 5.4 Try another one. Read the following passage and write a summary.

Water—the Great Mover

The rocks that form the earth's surface are being broken down constantly by weathering.* New soil is slowly forming. The deepest soils, then, should be found in mountain areas where exposed source rocks are most abundant. But this is not the case. The deepest soils are found in lowlands, often great distances from any mountains. The soil has been moved—and the single most important agent in the movement of soil over long distances is running water. As water accumulates on hills and mountains from rain or melting snow, it moves downhill. As it moves it picks up loose soil and debris.

In a previous investigation you observed the effects of shaking water and sand together in a bottle. When you stopped shaking the bottle the water did not stop moving immediately. Typically, the water continued to swirl about for a few seconds until friction within the water and against the sides of the container gradually brought it to a standstill. At the same time, the suspended material was settling out. The first particles to settle, while the water was still in fairly rapid motion, were the heavier ones. As the water moved less and less rapidly, finer and still finer particles settled.

This behavior is similar to what happens in nature. The more rapidly a stream flows, the more suspended material it can carry. When the stream is flowing slowly, less material can be held in suspension. As a result, the amount of material that a stream or river transports is not constant through the year.

Generally, streams tend to erode (wear away) banks and beds most actively in their headwaters, to transport material throughout their lengths, and to deposit material near their mouths. The degree of erosion, transportation, and deposition depends upon how rapidly the water moves.

Check your summary with the one found in Appendix B.

Does the summary have the following characteristics?

1. It is one fourth to one third the length of the original.

2. It is clear and easy to understand.

3. It contains all the main ideas that are in the original.

4. It does not contain any ideas that are not in the original.

5. It is written in your own words as much as possible.

---

* "Water—The Great Mover" from INTERACTION OF EARTH AND TIME, by Abraham, Chanedy, Moores and Swift. © 1979 by Rand McNally & Company. Used by Permission.

Why Should You Use Abbreviations?

Notes need to be an accurate record of information. Anything to shorten your notes is helpful as long as you can read and understand them later. Several ways to use abbreviations are:

1. Include only useful and important information.

   Statement: The people have a right to clean air, pure water, and to the preservation of the natural, scenic, historic, and aesthetic values of the environment.

   Shortened passage: People have rights to clean air, pure water and beautiful country.

2. Use symbols whenever possible.

   Listed are some common symbols:

=	Equal
≠	Unequal
e.g.	For example
i.e.	In other words
&	And
>	Greater than
<	Less than
etc.	And so forth
↑	Up
↓	Down

3. Abbreviate words.

   Abbreviate words like the following ones.

biology	bio	history	hist
chemistry	chem	home economics	home ec
education	educ	dollar sign	$
United States	U.S.	nickel	5c
Extra terrestrial	E.T.	Los Angeles International Airport	LAX

4. Leave out unnecessary words.

   Statement: Too often notes are written and then ignored until weeks later when test time is close.

   Shortened passage: Notes are written, ignored until test time.

Turn to page 59 in your *Student Activity Booklet* and complete Activity 5.2.

How Do You Handle Longer Passages?

Now that you have had an opportunity to work on the various skills in notetaking, we want you to work on several longer textbook passages. These will be similar to the work you are now doing in your classes. By completing these exercises, you will have the type of practice that will help you do a good job of taking notes from your textbooks. On these activities feel free to *underline, highlight,* and *write marginal notes* on the pages. While you can't do these in your regular books, you can practice these skills in your student activity booklet.

Turn to page 61 in your *Student Activity Booklet* and complete Activities 5.3 and 5.4.

You are now ready to apply these notetaking skills to your classes. Begin taking notes in one subject for one week. After that, add another subject each week until you have them all. By applying the notetaking system in your school work, you should begin to see good results.

Summary

This chapter has given you a method of taking notes from lectures and textbooks. The Summary Sheet System shows the relationship between the notes, the recall column, and the summary statement. The notes represent the main ideas and details presented in the passage. The recall column has questions about your notes. The summary statement maintains the meaning of the material and is restated in your own words as much as possible. This system will help put information into long term memory.

Now that you have completed this chapter, take a few minutes to check yourself on the material covered. Complete the checklist found on page 69 in your *Student Activity Booklet*. (Activity 5.5)

Chapter 6
Mapping: A Visual Way to Organize Your School Work

Everyone learns in a way which works for them. Mapping is a strategy you can use to organize your school work. You can use mapping for your lecture notes or the materials you read. Through mapping, you will have a better chance of getting information into long-term memory.

What is your SSQ on Mapping? To find out your SSQ turn to page 71 in your *Student Activity Booklet* and complete the checklist. (Activity 6.0)

What Is a Map?

A map is a *word picture* of ideas that is much like a road map. A road map gives you a picture of an area. It provides an overview of the land and it points out the major routes. A map of your school work is the same thing. It gives you, in picture form and on one page, all the important information (main ideas) as well as all of the details of an entire chapter!

What Does a Map Look Like?

You have just completed a chapter in science on air pollution. A map of this information might look like this:

EXAMPLE 6.1

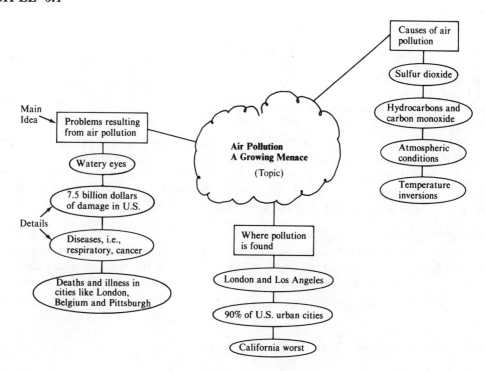

45

Notice the *TOPIC* "Air Pollution—A Growing Menace" is attached to three (3) *MAIN IDEAS*. Under each of the three main ideas are *DETAILS* that help to support these points. You now have a visual picture of the chapter on air pollution. From this map you can study for tests and complete your assignments. Won't it be great to have one page to review rather than pages and pages of notes? Try it!

What Are the Steps in Mapping?

You already know how to find the main idea in reading selections or your notes. In preparing your map, do the following steps:

(1) Read the material and find the topic. Write the topic on your paper and put a circle around it.

(2) Organize and categorize the main ideas under the topic. These are the major points that support the topic. Usually these are the black bold headings in the chapter. Other clues might include the use of italics, numbers, and clue words such as first, second, another point, and in addition.

(3) Carefully read the material under each main idea for the details. The number of details you use will vary from person to person. Just be sure you have enough details. They help you remember the most important parts of the topic and main ideas.

Once you have completed your map of this topic, you have organized your material for further study. Thus mapping helps you:

(1) organize information.
(2) retain information.
(3) relate main ideas to one another.
(4) study the information.
(5) review for your tests.

How Can You Make a Map?

There are three steps in making a map. First, we need to determine the topic. Look at the title. Does it announce the topic? If not, read the following short article. What is the topic of this passage?

Our American Coins

A penny for your thoughts. . . .
My two cents' worth. . . .
Don't take any wooden nickels!
This car will stop on a dime.

You have met these sayings before, of course. They are part of our everyday language. You can probably think of others which mention American coins.

It is true that these coins won't buy so much now as they once did. But, the sayings show that coins have always been important to us. And they always will be—unless we change to shells or sunflower seeds or something!

Importance of Coins

Every day we use coins in many different ways. We use them in candy machines and in telephone booths. We use them on the bus and in the store. We use coins to buy stamps and hot dogs and many other little things. If we have enough coins, we can even buy some of the bigger things.

—Adapted from *Our American Coins*, U.S. Government Printing Office

Coins always seem to be there for us to spend. We don't think much about what they mean or where they come from. But they can tell us a lot about our own country, past and present.

Coins in Early America

In this country, before it became the United States, there were many kinds of coins. There were coins from England, Spain, France, Holland, and Germany. People using one kind of money were doing business with people using another kind. They had to figure out, for example, what a Dutch coin was worth in English money, or what a Spanish coin was worth in French money. Sometimes there were mix-ups.

United States Mint

After the American Revolution, things changed. We felt we should all be using the same kind of money. So in 1792 Congress passed the laws needed for making American coins.

A United States Mint was set up to make, or mint, the new coins. The first Mint was in Philadelphia. It made copper cents and half cents.

Later other Mints were set up in Denver and San Francisco. The main office for all the Mints is in Washington, D.C. This office and all the Mints are part of the United States Treasury Department.

Shape of Coins

Coins are usually round so that they won't wear holes in people's pockets. Long ago, coins were carried in little bags with draw-string closings. The string let people tie the moneybag to a belt. Clothing didn't always have lots of pockets, and women didn't always carry purses.

Another reason for the round shape today is vending machines. Round coins go into the slots easily.

Sizes of Coins

The sizes of our coins today are all decided by law. Mostly they follow early Greek and Roman sizes. It is necessary for coins to be the right size. If they are too small, they can be easily lost or overlooked. If they are too big, they will be difficult to use and carry. You can imagine how it would be to carry around coins half the size of a dime, or coins three times larger than a half dollar.

Marks and Mottoes

Certain interesting marks and sayings, or mottoes, can be found on our coins. For example, a coin made in the Denver Mint has a D as its mintmark. The San Francisco Mint uses an S. Philadelphia has no mintmark.

By law, every U.S. coin has the Latin motto E PLURIBUS UNUM on one side. It means ONE OUT OF MANY. We are one country made out of many states and many peoples.

Also on every coin you will find the motto IN GOD WE TRUST. This was begun on some coins in 1864, during the War Between the States. Now, by law, it is put on all U.S. coins.

Certain coins, such as the Eisenhower dollar with Apollo 11, have great stories behind them. To learn more, write for the booklet *Our American Coins*. The price is twenty-five cents. Write to the Superintendent of Documents, U.S. Government Printing Office, Washington D.C., 20402.

EXERCISE 6.0 It is obvious the article is about "Our American Coins." So the topic is AMERICAN COINS. Take a sheet of paper and place the words "American Coins" on the paper. Circle the words. This is your topic.

Second, you want to find the main ideas. Remember, one of the clues to look for is the black bold headings or subheadings found in a reading selection. In this article, how many main ideas do you find? On the sheet of paper where your topic is listed, place the main ideas you find in the passage around the topic.

If you listed the following six main ideas, you have them all. They are:

1. Importance of Coins
2. Coins in Early America
3. United States Mint
4. Shape of Coins
5. Sizes of Coins
6. Marks and Mottoes

Make a box for each of these main ideas and place them around the topic you have already identified.

Your map should look something like this one. Make sure you have all six main ideas around the topic.

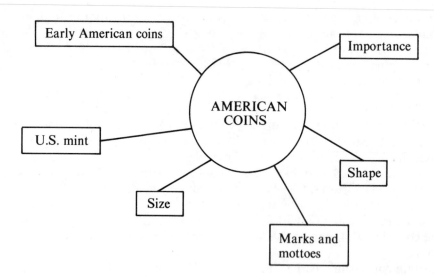

Now, go back over the passage and list all the details for each main idea. List them under the six main ideas.

EXAMPLE 6.2

Compare your map with the following one. Remember, you do not need to have exactly the same details. But you should have enough details to help you remember the important points under each main idea. Take a look!

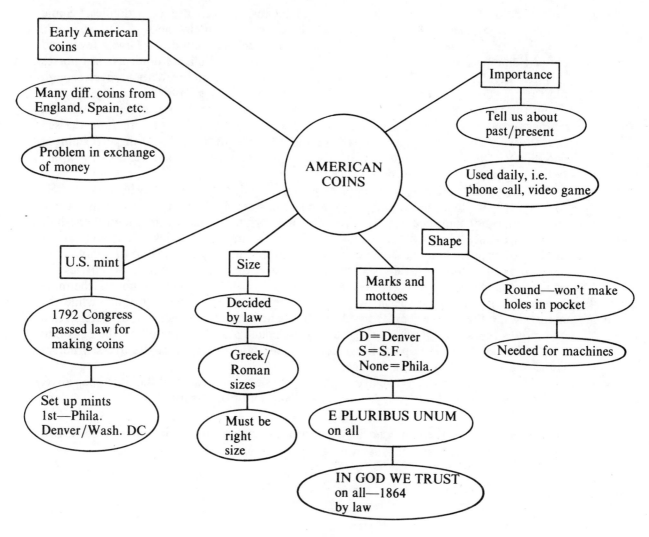

EXERCISE 6.1 Try mapping an article yourself. Read the following passage, take notes, and make a map of this information on a blank sheet of paper.

A Horse of a Different Color

Sea horses first became known long ago because of their use as medicines.* Some people thought they could be used to cure baldness or pains in the side. Other people thought that if a live sea horse were dipped in oil of roses it would drive away fever and chills. Some people even used sea horses in a love potion. Well, we don't use sea horses this way anymore. However, they are still unusual fish to see and read about, even though most people don't normally think of them as fish. They have gills for breathing, a dorsal fin on the back, and small fins on the front. These fins move the sea horse through the water, and at full speed they beat 35 times each second. To change direction, the sea horse jerks its head to change its balance much like a diver might do in performing a complicated dive off a springboard. If the sea horse doesn't want to move, it can wrap its tail around a piece of seaweed and stay there.

Although the sea horse can move its fins rapidly, it really cannot swim very fast. So to catch the live food that it eats, the sea horse has developed a mouth that has jet-like suction and pinpoint accuracy. If a young brine shrimp swims within one and one-half inches of the sea horse's mouth, it is sucked into the mouth so quickly that you cannot even see it happen. One sea horse can eat as many as 3600 brine shrimp in a day.

One of the strangest things about sea horses is that the male sea horse carries the eggs in a kangaroolike pouch until they hatch. To get the eggs into the pouch, the male and female go through a special way of courting behavior. They "hold tails" while the male bows to the female repeatedly. As he bows, he pumps his pouch full of water. Then he empties the water through a tiny hole in the pouch and the female lays the eggs into this hole. The eggs develop in this pouch, and in eight to ten days, the live sea horses come out of the tiny hole, one by one.

Many magazines advertise live sea horses for sale. They can be difficult to keep alive, but maybe you would like to try. They could be a lot of fun to study.

When you complete the map, check yours with the one on page 51 in your textbook. Did you have the same topic, main ideas, and details? If not, check back in the article.

*Biological Sciences Curriculum Study. The Colorado College, Colorado Springs, CO 80903.

EXAMPLE 6.3

Did you have enough detail to help you understand each main idea?

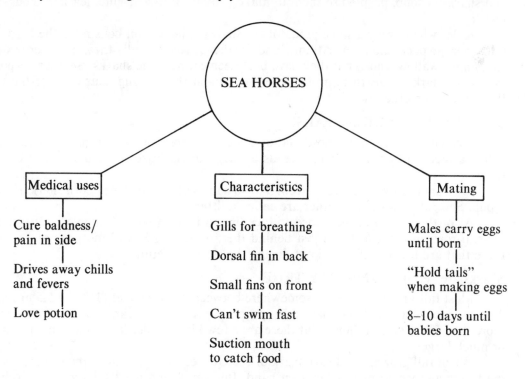

EXERCISE 6.2   Now you are ready to complete a longer story. Read the story. On a sheet of paper take notes. Be sure you include a summary statement of your notes. After you have your notes, make a map of this story from your notes. Next, check your notes and map with the ones provided on page 54. Now enjoy the story about sharks.

Sharks
by R. Newton

Ever since people first gazed out upon the sea, they have been fascinated by sharks.* Many stories about sharks have been told, some true, many false. How true are some of the stories you may have heard about sharks? Let's look at some of them and see.

All sharks are man-eaters. FALSE

Very few people are attacked by sharks each year, and only about a dozen of the over 250 different kinds of sharks are known ever to have attacked humans. Among these are the great white, tiger, lemon, mako, dusky, bull, and the strangest-looking of all sharks, the hammerhead.

More than any other, the great white shark has earned the name "man-eater." It is the third largest, reaching a length of over 36 feet (11m.). It will attack and eat almost anything, including humans.

Sharks live only in the warm parts of the ocean. FALSE

Some kinds of sharks are at home swimming under the ice of the Arctic Ocean. Others fin along in warm tropical seas. Sharks can be found in all the oceans of the world. Some kinds spend most of their lives close to shore and others far out to sea.

Sharks live in some of the big rivers of Australia, Africa, Asia, and South America. There are even sharks in one of the large freshwater lakes in Central America!

Sharks have no enemies. FALSE

People are the greatest predators of sharks. Besides using sharks to make fish sticks and shark-fin soup, people use them to make fish oil, fertilizer, glue, leather goods, and jewelry.

Killer whales may also be predators of sharks. These giant cousins of the porpoises hunt in large packs along the Atlantic and Pacific Coasts. Usually they attack prey small enough to swallow whole, but they have been seen eating large sharks. Smaller porpoises may butt sharks to death to protect themselves and their young. But most of the time they leave each other alone.

Sharks lay eggs. TRUE and FALSE

Some do. Some don't. Those that do lay eggs deposit them in a thick, rubbery case called a mermaid's purse. Long threads anchor the egg cases to underwater weeds or rocks.

Most sharks give live birth—from 5 to 60 babies at a time. A newborn shark is called a pup. Several pups born together are called a litter.

At birth each pup is equipped to face life on its own with a complete set of teeth. Several rows of extra teeth lie just behind the first set. They will move up and replace those that are broken off or fall out during the shark's lifetime.

Sharks are very large. MOSTLY TRUE

Most full-grown sharks are somewhere between 4 and 18 feet (1.2 and 5.5 m.) long. The common dogfish shark that many people catch while ocean fishing seldom grows more than 5 feet (1.5 m.) long. But there are a few kinds of sharks that are much smaller or much larger.

When full grown, the dwarf shark of the Gulf of Mexico is only about 5 inches (13 cm.) long and would fit in your open hand. But you would need a huge crane to lift a whale shark out of the water. The whale shark is the world's largest fish. It may reach a length to 60 feet (18 m.) and weigh more than 15 tons. The second largest fish, the basking shark, may be as long as 50 feet (15 m.).

Sharks are slow moving. FALSE

It is true that some sharks are so sluggish that you might wonder how they catch their prey. But most sharks can cruise at 5 to 10 miles (8 to 16 km.) an hour and, if the need arises, zip through the water at up to 30 miles (48 km.) an hour for short distances. That isn't slow!

Sharks are able to smell blood in the water. TRUE

Sharks are first drawn to noises that seem unusual. A struggling fish or other animal sends irregular sounds through the water. These may attract sharks in a hurry from as far as a mile (1.6km.) away.

Next they rely on their keen sense of smell to find their meals. They can detect small amounts of blood from up to half a mile (0.8 km.) away.

When a shark gets near enough, its eyesight usually takes over. It may swim in circles around its prey, getting closer and closer. Or it may dart straight in. At the last instant a shark may rely on tiny sense organs around its mouth to pick up electrical signals from the prey. The shark uses these to aim its killing bite.

Sharks must turn over to eat. FALSE

Sharks may turn on their sides or even upside down to eat if they so desire, but they certainly don't have to. Sharks can feed in their normal swimming position as easily as any other fish. They simply thrust forward their lower jaws, complete with sharp, jagged teeth, and take a bite.

Sharks have an acid in their stomachs that will dissolve anything. FALSE

It is true that such strange things as old rubber tires, tin cans, metal pans, and glass bottles have been found in the stomachs of sharks. But they get rid of these items by throwing them up, not by digesting them.

Sharks have huge appetites. MOSTLY TRUE

The giant whale sharks and basking sharks feed almost entirely on small fish and tiny animals and plants called plankton. Swimming open-mouthed near the surface, they strain great amounts of food from the water.

A few sharks gorge themselves on clams, mussels, and other shelled animals they find living on the sea floor.

By far the largest number of sharks are fish-eaters; they also may dine on seals, turtles, birds, and almost anything else that moves, including other sharks.

Sometimes a group of sharks will become so excited over their meal that they work themselves into a "feeding frenzy." When this happens, they will eat anything they can grab, even logs, a boat propeller, or another shark!

Some sharks add to their diet by eating garbage thrown overboard from ships. They have been known to follow ships for days looking for a handout.

Sharks differ from other fish. TRUE

For one thing, sharks do not have skeletons made of bones as do other fish. They have tough, grisly cartilage instead—the same kind of hard rubbery tissue you can feel at the end of your nose.

Most bony fish have flat, overlapping scales and are very slippery to hold. The scales on a shark's skin are like very tiny, hard teeth. They make the skin so rough that people in the past have used it for sandpaper.

A shark's mouth is located below its long snout, whereas the mouths of most bony fish are up front. On each side of a shark are 5 to 7 open gill slits behind the head. Most bony fish have a single gill opening each side, covered by a flap.

Bony fish have inside them a sac of gases called a swimbladder. This keeps them from sinking. Sharks don't have swimbladders. When they stop swimming they sink.

Sharks may live to an old age. UNKNOWN

Scientists can count the growth rings on the scales of a bony fish to tell its age, but this method doesn't work on the toothy scales of a shark. The age of sharks is just one of the many things we do not know about these sleek hunters of the sea.

Now that you have completed your notes on sharks, look at the notes provided. Are the essential parts of the notes similar? If not, look back and see where your notes are different from the model. Remember, you do not need to have the same detail, but the five main ideas need to be similar (True, False, True & False, Mostly True, and Unknown).

EXAMPLE 6.4   Notes

Recall Column	Notes
	Many Stories Told about Sharks, Some True, Many False

What are some false stories about sharks?	*All sharks eat people—False*
	    of 250 kinds only about 12 attack people
	    some that do: great white, tiger, hammerhead

	Sharks live only in warm ocean—False
	    found in all oceans
	    warm and cold waters
	    fresh and salt waters

	Sharks don't have enemies—False
	    men kill sharks for many uses, food, fertilizer, etc.
	    killer whales may eat sharks
	    porpoises kill sharks to protect young

	Sharks are slow moving—False
	    few are very slow
	    many swim 5 to 10 m.p.h.
	    can swim fast as 30 m.p.h.

	Sharks must turn over to eat—False can eat in any position they want to

	Sharks have acid in stomachs that will digest anything—False
	    don't digest things such as tires, cans
	    throw them up, instead

What are some true stories about sharks?	*Sharks can smell blood—True*
	    first attracted to struggle by sound
	    then can smell blood up to ½ mile away
	    when close enough, shark sees prey

	Sharks differ from other fish—True
	    don't have bones, have cartilage
	    have rough skin with teeth-like scales
	    mouth under snout instead of up front
	    have 5 to 7 gill slits instead of one
	    don't have swimbladder like most fish

What are some true/false stories about sharks?	*Sharks lay eggs—True and False*
	    some sharks lay eggs on rubbery cases called
	        "mermaid's purse"
	    most sharks give live birth
	        "litters" of 4 to 60 "pups"
	        "pups" can take care of themselves

EXAMPLE 6.4—Continued

Recall Column	Notes

What are some mostly true stories about sharks?	*Sharks are very large—Mostly True*
	    most adults 4 to 18 feet
	    few small sharks—dwarf shark 5 in. long
	    some very large—whale shark 60 ft. long
	
	Sharks have huge appetites—Mostly True
	    eat almost anything that moves
	        some of the biggest sharks eat only small plankton
	        most eat other fish
	        some eat shellfish, seals, birds, turtles
	        some eat garbage from ships
	        can work into "feeding frenzy" and eat anything

What are some unknown stories about sharks?	*Sharks may live to an old age—Unknown* scientists can't count growth rings Summary Some stories people tell about sharks are true. Many are false. The false stories are often based on misinformation about sharks. The types of sharks vary greatly in size, eating habits, habitat, appearance, and method of having young.

EXAMPLE 6.5

Look at the map that follows. Are the essential parts of the map similar? If not, look back and see where your map is different. Remember, you do not need to have the same detail. However, the five main ideas need to be the same.

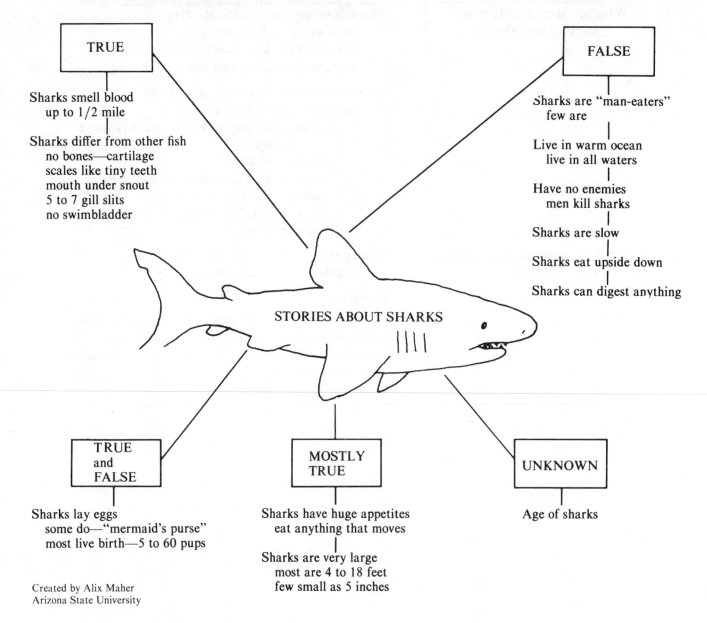

TRUE

Sharks smell blood
  up to 1/2 mile

Sharks differ from other fish
  no bones—cartilage
  scales like tiny teeth
  mouth under snout
  5 to 7 gill slits
  no swimbladder

FALSE

Sharks are "man-eaters"
  few are

Live in warm ocean
  live in all waters

Have no enemies
  men kill sharks

Sharks are slow

Sharks eat upside down

Sharks can digest anything

STORIES ABOUT SHARKS

TRUE and FALSE

Sharks lay eggs
  some do—"mermaid's purse"
  most live birth—5 to 60 pups

MOSTLY TRUE

Sharks have huge appetites
  eat anything that moves

Sharks are very large
  most are 4 to 18 feet
  few small as 5 inches

UNKNOWN

Age of sharks

Created by Alix Maher
Arizona State University

Summary

Mapping is a way to organize your textbook notes, lecture notes, and other materials for later study. It gives you an opportunity to see how the parts fit together. Mapping can be used as a final step in preparing your material for study. It will give you a *picture* of the material you want to learn.

Now that you have completed this chapter, take a few minutes to check yourself on the material covered. Complete the checklist found on page 73 in your *Student Activity Booklet*. (Activity 6.1)

Chapter 7
Taking Tests

Tests are used to measure how much the student knows about a specific subject or area. A test can give the teacher and the student a lot of information in a short period of time. Tests can indicate the student's potential, thinking process, and future success.

Our society is test oriented. It is necessary to realize that tests will be given to you throughout our lives. In school or in your future job, you will face tests. Being adequately prepared is the best way to avoid the feeling of test anxiety. If you make a reasonable effort to prepare for tests, you usually have nothing to fear.

What is your SSQ on taking tests? To find out your SSQ turn to page 75 in your *Student Activity Booklet* and complete the checklist. (Activity 7.0)

Do You Have to Take Tests?

It seems there is a test for every topic and situation which involves you. Often you do not like taking tests and put off thinking about this until the last minute. A better attitude is to think of tests as an evaluation, a way to measure how much you know. Don't *procrastinate!* Tests are here to stay.

How Often Will Tests Be Given?

This will usually depend on the individual teacher, the course, the situation, and the goals the teacher wants to accomplish. Tests may be every day, once a week, twice a month or whenever appropriate. Whenever they are given, the goal is to be prepared and do your best.

How Do You Prepare for Tests?

One way to prepare for tests is to use this equation: LISTENING + THINKING + WORKING + PATIENCE = SUCCESS. Next, is to begin taking good notes the first day of class. If necessary, review the notetaking techniques suggested in Chapter 5. Developing questions for the recall column and writing a summary for your notes will also help you get ready for tests. Reviewing your notes frequently will help you store new information in long-term memory. Mapping the notes taken in lectures and from the text will also give you an organizational picture of the material and make learning easier. (Refer back to chapter 6 for a review of the mapping technique.) Finally, reviewing nightly will help you learn the material without cramming the night before the test.

What Questions Can You Ask Yourself When Studying for Tests?

Specific questions can be asked when reviewing the material for a test. The questions are:

1. What information does the author think is important?
2. Do I get these ideas when I read the material?
3. Do I know the important topics and can I verbalize them?
4. How can I apply these ideas in my life?

What Are Some General Test Taking Tips?

Here are some tips that may help you take tests. Some of these tips you may already be doing. The tips are:

1. *Overlearn the material.* If you overlearn the material, you will reduce test anxiety. Avoid cramming by studying nightly over a longer period of time.

2. *Be on time* to the test. Getting there late will increase your anxiety just as much as being there too early. Ignore the others around you who are worrying. This will only increase your anxiety level.

3. *Write your name* on the paper the minute you get the test.

4. *Write down any information* you have learned to help you remember specific information when taking essay notes. From these points write the answers to the questions.

5. *Read, don't skim, the directions.* They may be different for each part of the test. If possible, circle the key words in the directions so you are sure to complete each section correctly.

6. *Manage your time well.* Determine which sections of the test have the most points. Spend the right amount of time necessary to answer these questions. The true-false or multiple choice questions could be done first, saving plenty of time for the more difficult questions. If they are essay questions, take care you plan enough time for each question fully and carefully.

7. *Skip questions you are unsure of or questions where the answers don't come quickly to mind.* Don't dwell on these. Go on to the next question. You can come back to the ones you don't answer if time permits.

8. *Re-check your work* for errors.

9. *Ask to see your corrected test.* Look at the errors you made. This will make you test-wise in the future.

What Kinds of Tests Are There?

There are two types of tests: *essay* and *objective.* Essay tests require information to be written in paragraph form. Objective tests are short answer tests like: completion, multiple choice, matching, and true-false. Preparing for the two types of tests is somewhat different.

What Are Some Tips in Answering True-False Questions?

Several tips include:

1. Assume the statement is true unless you can establish it as false. It is easier to write a true statement than a false one.

2. A statement is false if any part of it is false.

3. Absolute statements tend to be false. Watch for the words: *never, always, none, only, all, best, invariably.* These statements are usually false. On the other hand, words like: *many, most, some, generally, frequently,* and *often* are usually used in true statements.

4. Watch out for the word *NOT.* It completely changes the meaning of the statement.

5. If you are not sure what the question is about, ask your teacher for clarification.

EXERCISE 7.0   Listed are some true-false statements. Use the tips listed above to help you answer them. On a sheet of paper number from one to five. Place a T next to the number if the statement is true or an F if the statement is false.

1. You should never skip words while reading silently.

2. The recall column in the notetaking system is used to recopy detailed information.

3. Good, effective listeners tend to pay more attention to details and this helps to make short–term memory more important than long—term memory for time management.

4. Events calendars are always more important than the master calendar.

5. Usually people forget more right after being exposed to information.

Check your answers with those found in Appendix B.

What Are Some Tips in Answering Multiple–Choice Questions?

1. Read the "stem" of the question: "The largest number of sharks eat," and try to answer it before you read the choices given. After you decide on your answer, compare it to the possible answers and select the one most like yours.

2. If you are to read long passages and answer questions about the material, read the question stems before reading the material. That will help you find what you are looking for faster and easier.

3. Do not be afraid to change your answers on a multiple choice test if you have a good reason. A myth still survives that you should stick to your original choice. Studies show that most students are at least twice as likely to change an incorrect answer to a correct one.

4. Be logical. Logical reasoning can help you see through the good distractors and locate the correct answer.

5. If the answers are a list of dates or numbers, you can usually eliminate the lowest and the highest number.

6. Watch out for the word NOT. It completely changes the meaning of the stem.

7. Absolute words like *all, none, never, always, constantly,* and *usually* make the answer untrue and should be eliminated as distractors.

8. Answers that are combinations of possible answers are usually right. An example: a. potatoes b. carrots c. potatoes and carrots d. onions. C is probably the correct answer, because it combines several answers.

EXERCISE 7.1   Here are some multiple–choice questions. Use the tips we give you to help answer them. On a sheet of paper number from one to five. Place the letter of the best answer next to number for each question.

1. World War II began in:
    a. 1934
    b. 1939
    c. 1941
    d. 1945
2. Which was *not* a cause of the Civil War?
    a. slavery
    b. taxation without representation
    c. state's rights
    d. abolition

3. Medicines bought without prescriptions can be more harmful than good because:
   a. they may treat the symptoms not the causes
   b. they are not recommended by doctors
   c. there is too great a variety available
   d. average people cannot make these decisions
4. When giving speeches, students can be most successful when they:
   a. use one source
   b. use a variety of sources
   c. base the speech on original thought and research
   d. cite personal opinion
5. The difficulty of the reading material can be usually determined by looking at the:
   a. words
   b. sentences
   c. paragraph
   d. words and sentences

Check your answers with those found in Appendix B.

What Are Some Tips in Answering Essay Questions?

Closely examine the words of the question. Commonly used words include: compare, define, explain, describe, discuss, summarize. Each of these words has a different meaning and requires a different answer. To make sure you understand the meaning of these "direction" words, study the following definitions:

a. Compare:	Look at the characteristics, qualities of the two items: Usually you are asked to emphasize the similarities and/or the differences of the characteristics or qualities of the two items.
b. Define:	Clear, concise, meanings. Keep in mind the class to which the item belongs and whatever makes it different from other classes.
c. Describe:	Tell about the item: its characteristics, qualities, distinctive markings. Recount, sketch out, or relate in narrative form.
d. Discuss:	Examine and analyze carefully. Present considerations for and against the problems or issues involved. This calls for a complete and detailed answer.
e. Explain:	Clarify and interpret the material. It is best to state "how or why" and reconcile any differences in opinion that exist. State causes. The aim is to make the conditions plain and clear.
f. Summarize:	Condense the information. State only the main topics or facts. Omit all the details, illustrations, and elaboration.

You may not like answering essay tests because you are required to write the answer in paragraph form. If you do not write well, you may be worried about this fact. The only way to become a good essay test writer is to practice writing answers to questions that might appear on the test. Once you get to the test, consider these tips:

1. *Jot down* all the facts you know about the subject right away.
2. *Briefly outline* the answer by organizing the facts in a logical way.
3. *Begin your answer with an introduction, end with a summary.* The introduction will state the main points to be made in the answer. The summary will restate the points made in the answer.
4. *Logically construct the body of the answer, moving from the general to the specific.* That will give the body strength and order. If the answer is chronological, be sure to get the dates in the right time order. Write as if your reader knew nothing about the subject. Be clear and concise on all points and include as much information as possible.

5. *Reread the answer.* You may have thought faster than you can write and words have been left out. Spell words correctly and punctuate appropriately so your meaning is clear.

6. *Write carefully.* Your penmanship is important on an essay question. Poor handwriting can make grading a difficult test. If it is not easily read, you may lose points.

EXERCISE 7.2   Now try these questions. From your study of the material in this book, answer the following essay questions on a sheet of paper.

(1) Summarize why it is necessary to know how to study.

(2) Define what it means to be a flexible reader.

(3) Discuss the PREP Study System.

(4) Compare mapping and notetaking.

Check your answers with those found in Appendix B.

EXERCISE 7.3   To practice making questions for tests, read each of the following passages. Write one true-false statement, one multiple choice question, and one essay question. Give the answer for each question.

(1)   *Sleeping Gear*

The basic bedroll consists of a waterproof ground cover, a foam pad or rubber air mattress, a sleeping bag, and a water-resistant cover.

Ground covers must be waterproof and free of punctures; both treated tarpaulin and nylon will keep moisture from seeping into sleeping pads. Backpackers favor foam pads because they're lightweight, roll up tightly, and provide good insulation from cold ground and because, best of all, perhaps, you don't have to blow them up or worry about their going flat during that night.

Down-filled sleeping bags are still the greatest, but they are expensive; on the other hand, bags insulated with a polyester fiber approach down bags in warmth and compactness and cost only about one-third as much. Unless you plan to spend much of your time in the Arctic or at high altitudes, bags insulated with polyester might be the best way to reduce costs without reducing quality.

Check your questions with those found in Appendix B.

(2)   *Sharks Have Huge Appetites*

The giant whale sharks and basking sharks feed almost entirely on small fish and tiny animals and plants called *plankton.* Swimming open-mouthed near the surface, they strain great amounts of food from the water.

A few sharks gorge themselves on clams, mussels, and other shelled animals they find living on the sea floor.

By far the largest number of sharks are fish-eaters; they also may dine on seals, turtles, birds, and almost anything else that moves, including other sharks.

Sometimes a group of sharks will become so excited over their meal that they work themselves into a "feeding frenzy." When this happens, they will eat anything they can grab, even logs, a boat propeller or another shark!

Some sharks add to their diet by eating garbage thrown overboard from ships. They have been known to follow ships for days looking for a handout.

Check your questions with those found in Appendix B.

(3)   *Smoke Jumpers*

    The smoke jumper's job is to break the "fire triangle." The three sides of the fire triangle are heat, fuel, and air. When firemen remove any one of these three things, the triangle is broken. Then the fire goes out. Most of the time the smoke jumpers try to remove the fuel from the triangle. They do this by cutting a line, or fuel break, around the fire. They use power saws, axes, and shovels to remove grass, needles, and other forest fuels. When all the fuel has been removed around the edge of a fire, the triangle is broken.

Check your questions with those found in Appendix B.

(4)   *A Bush Pilot*

    No one understands the difficulties—and the excitement—of flying in glacier lands better than Don Sheldon. Sheldon has been flying in Alaska for over 23 years, and he has run through 45 aircraft. But he has never lost a passenger. And he has always been able to walk away from his landings—although some of them have been a little on the exciting side.

    Much of Sheldon's flying is with groups of mountain climbers. Sheldon flies groups to their base camps and also delivers supplies to them. He often has 15 to 20 different climbing parties to watch over during the season. And, of course, emergency trips are needed from time to time as trouble strikes one group or another. So he spends much of his summer landing on glaciers and uneven slopes of all sorts.

    Flying in glacier land calls for a special kind of pilot. A bush pilot has to be able to make repairs on his own plane. He must be willing to do his own oil changes and refueling. He must be able to fly through blinding snowstorms with no landmarks in sight. He's got to be tough enough to lick the weather and the wild country. And if he is forced down, he must know how to survive. Not all pilots—not even good ones—can handle this kind of flying.

Check your questions with those found in Appendix B.

    Share your questions with your classmates. See how many questions you have alike/different.

Summary

    By preparing for tests in a structured way, you will most likely improve your performance and reduce test anxiety. Be sure to use the study strategies learned in this book. Develop a positive attitude about tests. Make sure you are ready. When taking tests remember to: (1) read directions carefully, (2) budget your time, (3) answer the easiest questions first, and (4) control any excess anxiety. Be neat. Always write something on every essay item. Develop a system for dealing with essay questions including: (1) review the test, (2) budget your time, (3) select an essay question first, (4) write a rough outline except for a brief essay, and (5) write your response in an organized, logical way.

    Now that you have completed this chapter, take a few minutes to check yourself on the material covered. Complete the checklist found on page 77 in your *Student Activity Booklet*. (Activity 7.1)

Comprehension Reading Selections

You will be reading a number of readings of various lengths during this course. Your teacher will give you instructions for working on these selections.

The steps you are to follow while reading these selections are as follows:

1) Preview the material briefly. Read the title. Read the first and last paragraph. This should take only a few seconds of your reading time.

2) Write down your starting time on a sheet of paper. (If your teacher is timing everyone in class, you won't need to do this.

3) When you have completed reading the selection, write your ending time on the sheet of paper.

4) Next, complete the essay questions and the vocabulary questions on a blank sheet of paper.

5) Check your answers with the answer key. If you missed any items, check back in reading and see if you can figure out why you made the mistake.

6) Figure out your reading time. Look on the Time Conversion Chart for your reading rate.

7) Record your vocabulary scores and your reading time on the Comprehension Record Chart in your *Student Activity Booklet* on page 79.

CHANGING WEATHER

From day to day the sky keeps changing.* Sometimes the sky is blue. The clouds are white and fluffy. At other times the sky is dark. The clouds are big and black. All these changes make up the weather. The weather changes from day to day.

Look out of the window. Observe the sky for a few minutes. Are there clouds in the sky? What do the clouds look like? Are the clouds in the sky moving?

Plan to observe the sky each morning. Observe it each noon and in the afternoon. Make observations about the clouds. How much of the sky is covered by clouds? What do the clouds look like?

There are three main kinds of clouds. Think of the clouds you have seen. Can you pick out three kinds of clouds? What shapes did you see? Each kind of cloud has a different shape.

The scientist gives names to the three kinds of clouds. The three kinds are *cirrus* clouds, *stratus* clouds, and *cumulus* clouds.

The cirrus clouds are white. Sometimes they look like silk. Their shape is like a feather. The picture shows some cirrus clouds.

The stratus clouds form a layer across the sky. The different kinds of stratus clouds all look like fog. But the fog is not on the ground.

The cumulus clouds are thick and puffy. Most of these clouds have flat bottoms. They usually rise high in the sky. The top of the cloud is round. It is shaped like a hill. Study the cumulus clouds. You will see the different shapes.

Clouds are made of little drops of water. You can see the drops float in the air. Sunbeams strike the drops of water and light them up. The cloud looks white with the sun shining on it.

We are going to find out how clouds form. To do this we must learn about *evaporation* and *condensation*. Let's do experiments to find out about evaporation and condensation. Rub a wet sponge over a chalkboard. What happens? The water disappears from the chalkboard. The water goes into the air. We call this disappearance evaporation. We cannot see the water after it evaporates. The water in the air is called water vapor. There is water vapor in the air around you. You cannot see it. But the water vapor is there.

Put a teaspoon of water in two heatproof pie plates. Put one of the pie plates on a hot plate. Turn on the heat. From which pie plate does the water evaporate first? The water on the hot plate evaporates first. Heat speeds up the evaporation. Hot water evaporates faster than cold water.

Water evaporates from rivers, lakes, and bays. It evaporates from the oceans. The sun gives off heat. The heat from the sun causes the water to evaporate. The water from rivers, lakes, bays, and the oceans becomes water vapor.

Feel the outside of a tin can. It should be dry. Fill the tin can with ice. Does the outside of the can stay dry? The ice in the can makes the tin can cold. The water vapor in the air is cooled when it touches the cold can. The water vapor then changes back to drops of water we can see. The change from water we cannot see to water we can see is condensation.

The sun shines through a cloud. The sun lights up all the water drops in the cloud. This makes the cloud look white and fluffy. Sometimes a cloud begins to look dark. The cloud is dark because the water drops are getting big. The colder it gets, the bigger the water drops become. Big water drops stop the sun from shining through the cloud. The big drops get in the way of the sunlight. They make a shadow. The cloud looks dark. Remember the water drops in a cloud are floating in the air. A dark shadow in a cloud means the water drops are getting big. The water drops may get too big to float. Then they fall from the cloud.

*Reprinted by permission.

Water drops that fall from a cloud are called rain. All rain comes from a cloud. Dark clouds in the sky often bring rain. Sometimes we do not see a cloud when it rains. The cloud is too far away for us to see. The wind has carried the rain far from the cloud. Have you ever seen rain with no clouds around?

Essay Questions: On a sheet of paper answer the following questions.

1. Describe one of the three kinds of clouds.
2. What cycle does water go through?
3. How does the weather affect your planning for the day?

Check your answers with those found in Appendix B.

Vocabulary Exercise: On a sheet of paper, place the letter of the best answer next to the number for each vocabulary word.

1. observe
   "Plan to observe the sky each morning."
   a. draw
   b. remember
   c. view
   d. ignore
2. main
   "There are three main kinds of clouds."
   a. normal
   b. different
   c. similar
   d. major
3. causes
   "The heat from the sun causes the water to evaporate."
   a. directs
   b. makes
   c. burns
   d. becomes
4. speeds
   "Heat speeds up the evaporation."
   a. slows
   b. hurries
   c. prevents
   d. starts

5. strike

"Sunbeams strike the drops of water and light them up."

   a. hits
   b. forces
   c. directs
   d. frees

6. carried

"The wind has carried the rain far from the cloud."

   a. moved
   b. transferred
   c. dropped
   d. evaporated

7. bays

"Water evaporates from rivers, lakes, and bays."

   a. puddles
   b. springs
   c. sea inlets
   d. standing water

Check your answers with those found in Appendix B.

Time Conversion Chart

Min:Sec	WPM	Min:Sec	WPM	Min:Sec	WPM	Min:Sec	WPM	Min:Sec	WPM
1:00	775	2:20	332	3:40	211	5:00	155	6:20	122
1:10	664	2:30	310	3:50	202	5:10	150	6:30	119
1:20	581	2:40	291	4:00	194	5:20	145	6:40	116
1:30	517	2:50	274	4:10	186	5:30	141	6:50	113
1:40	465	3:00	258	4:20	179	5:40	137	7:00	111
1:50	423	3:10	245	4:30	172	5:50	133		
2:00	387	3:20	233	4:40	166	6:00	129		
2:10	358	3:30	221	4:50	160	6:10	125		

BUSH PILOT IN GLACIER LAND

When you hear the words bush pilot, do you think of Africa? Think of Alaska instead. Up there in our 50th state, bush pilots have opened up huge areas of wild country. Some 700 or so bush pilots deliver supplies, haul light freight, and carry passengers.

Bush pilots will go anywhere in weather that would ground even the sea gulls in other parts of the country. But the distances, the land, and the weather are all dangerous. The accident rate is high.

No one understands the difficulties—and the excitement—of flying in glacier lands better than Don Sheldon. Sheldon has been flying in Alaska for over 23 years, and he has run through 45 aircraft. But he has never lost a passenger. And he has always been able to walk away from his landings—although some of them have been a little on the exciting side.

Much of Sheldon's flying is with groups of mountain climbers. Sheldon flies groups to their base camps and also delivers supplies to them. He often has 15 to 20 different climbing parties to watch over during the season. And, of course, emergency trips are needed from time to time as trouble strikes one group or another. So he spends much of his summer landing on glaciers and uneven slopes of all sorts.

Flying in glacier land calls for a special kind of pilot. A bush pilot has to be able to make repairs on his own plane. He must be willing to do his own oil changes and refueling. He must be able to fly through blinding snowstorms with no landmarks in sight. He's got to be tough enough to lick the weather and the wild country. And if he is forced down, he must know how to survive. Not all pilots—not even good ones—can handle this kind of flying.

Sheldon's business is based in his home in the village of Talkeetna. He has a small fleet of bush planes parked outside and a floatplane bobbing on nearby Susitna River. Radio antennas seem to sprout from his house. His wife uses the radios to keep in touch with him and also with his mountain-climbing groups.

The business includes taking people on sightseeing trips. The two-hour sightseeing flight around Mt. McKinley is an exciting trip. McKinley sparkles in sunshine as the plane lifts from the strip beside the Sheldon home. The pilot flies over dozens of moose in swampy pastures and heads for Ruth Glacier. This mighty river of ice starts near sea level and rises to about 6,000 feet in just a few miles.

Near the base of McKinley, Sheldon points out a mountain cabin. He flew it in—in 14 trips—and put it up on land which he had bought from the state. He uses it for picnics, for ski parties, etc. Soon the passengers see the bright-colored tents which are the camps of the climbing parties.

Flying low over the glaciers on the way home, they see blue ice-water lakes flashing in the sun. Sheldon stops at various camps, checking on miners and trappers. Sometimes he delivers groceries, without charge, on these trips. He checks on some of his mountain-climbing parties, and his passengers often see a group, roped together, climbing an icy peak. He talks to them by radio (which he supplies to each group) and checks with his wife by radio.

Every flight with Sheldon is full of interest. People get a very good idea of what Alaska and its people are all about.

And every day is full of interest for Sheldon—even though it often begins at 5 a.m. and lasts until after dark. It's hard work, but he considers himself a lucky man. He is doing what he loves, and he loves where he is doing it.

*Reprinted from *Friends,* the Chevrolet-owner magazine.

Essay Questions: On a sheet of paper answer the following questions:

1. What skills must a bush pilot have to do this kind of flying?
2. Why are bush pilots important to Alaska?
3. What kind of training would you need to become a bush pilot?

Check your answers with those found in Appendix B.

Vocabulary Exercise: On a sheet of paper, place the letter of the best answer next to the number for each vocabulary word.

1. glacier
   "Flying in glacier land calls for a special kind of pilot."
   a. remote Alaskan wilderness
   b. heavy forests of tall pines
   c. moving ice and packed snow
   d. high, cold, altitudes at the Arctic circle

2. lick
   "He's got to be tough enough to lick the weather. . . ."
   a. beat
   b. enjoy
   c. change
   d. endure

3. emergency
   ". . . emergency trips are needed from time to time to help. . . ."
   a. planned
   b. exciting
   c. occasional
   d. crisis

4. ground
   "Bush pilots would go anywhere in weather that would ground even the sea gulls. . . ."
   a. blow off course
   b. stop from going
   c. cause accidents
   d. prepare to leave

5. survive
   ". . . and if he is forced down, he must know how to survive."
   a. repair damage to plane
   b. live without help or supplies
   c. call to be rescued
   d. land the plan safely

6. fleet
   "He has a small fleet of bush planes. . . ."
   a. number
   b. collection
   c. expensive
   d. worn out

7. base camps
   "Sheldon flies groups to their base camps. . . ."
   a. place where supplies are kept
   b. a training area
   c. place to buy supplies
   d. place near mountain tops where climbers meet

Check your answers with those found in Appendix B.

Time Conversion Chart

Min:Sec	WPM	Min:Sec	WPM	Min:Sec	WPM	Min:Sec	WPM	Min:Sec	WPM
1:00	790	2:40	296	4:20	182	6:00	132	7:40	103
1:10	677	2:50	279	4:30	176	6:10	128	7:50	101
1:20	593	3:00	263	4:40	169	6:20	125	8:00	99
1:30	527	3:10	249	4:50	163	6:30	122		
1:40	474	3:20	237	5:00	158	6:40	119		
1:50	431	3:30	226	5:10	153	6:50	116		
2:00	395	3:40	215	5:20	148	7:00	113		
2:10	365	3:50	206	5:30	144	7:10	110		
2:20	339	4:00	198	5:40	139	7:20	108		
2:30	316	4:10	190	5:50	135	7:30	105		

FRANKLIN THE SCIENTIST

Electricity was one of the things that interested Benjamin most. Not much was known about electricity at that time. But a man in the Netherlands had invented a jar in which electricity could be stored.

"I would like to know more about electricity," Benjamin said to his friends. "I would like to know about thunder and lightning, too. I wonder what makes lightning and what it can do. Do you suppose that lightning is electricity?"

"If lightning strikes you, it can kill you!" his friends warned him. This is true, but it did not worry Benjamin.

"I think we might be able to catch lightning and put it to work," he thought. "Men make the wind work for them; why not lightning?"

One day Benjamin said to his twenty-one-year-old son William, "When I was a boy, I used a kite to help me swim. I am going to use a kite to help me catch some lightning."

Benjamin waited until a summer day when a thunderstorm was near. Then he and William went to a shed in an open field. They carried a kite and string. There was a big brass key and a piece of silk ribbon tied to the end of the string.

"With these I am going to find out if lightning and electricity are the same," Benjamin said to his son. "When the kite is flying, I shall hold the ribbon and stand in the doorway of the shed. The ribbon will stay dry, even though the kite and string get wet in the rain."

High up in the sky the wind carried the kite. There came a boom of thunder in the distance. Suddenly there was a bright flash of lightning overhead.

"Watch the key, William, and see what happens!" cried Benjamin.

Sparks flashed at them from the brass key. Benjamin Franklin smiled happily. The sparks were gone in an instant. But he had found the answer to his question. Lightning *is* electricity.

"Electricity is very dangerous," said Benjamin. "But someday we may learn to make it useful, too."

To protect homes and barns from lightning, Benjamin invented the lightning rod. People who studied science were excited by Benjamin Franklin's discoveries. Now he was famous all over the world.

Franklin Helps His Country

Benjamin Franklin put his busy mind to work and solved other problems. When trouble arose between the thirteen colonies and Great Britain, his work became even more important.

In 1765 trouble came up with Great Britain over taxes. Great Britain decided that the American colonists should buy stamps and put them on everything that they sold. This would raise money for Great Britain.

"The Stamp Act is unfair!" cried the colonists. "This law should be changed. We must send one of our leading men to England to tell the King how we feel about this."

If any man could succeed in getting the Stamp Act changed, it was Benjamin Franklin. So he was chosen for this important trip. The next year, thanks to his help, the Stamp Act was removed. But Great Britain still said that the colonies would have to pay a tax on tea. Benjamin Franklin was very upset when news of the Boston Tea Party reached him in London several years later.

Benjamin Franklin stayed in England for ten years. All this time he was working for fair treatment of the thirteen American colonies. Wisely and calmly he did his best to prevent war between Great Britain and the colonies.

But when he finally sailed for Philadelphia, he had tears in his eyes. "Sooner or later we shall have war with Great Britain," he thought sadly.

*From TRAIL BLAZERS OF AMERICAN HISTORY, Revised Edition by Miriam E. Mason and William H. Cartwright, © Copyright, 1966, 1961, by Ginn and Company (Xerox Corporation). Used with permission.

He landed in Philadelphia in May. The first news he heard was that fighting had already begun at Lexington and Concord in Massachusetts.

"We shall fight until we are a free and independent nation," the colonists declared. "We'll write a paper to show the rest of the world what we are fighting for."

Benjamin Franklin was chosen to help write this important paper. It was called The Declaration of Independence, as you have learned. It was completed on July 4, 1776. That is why the fourth of July is called Independence Day.

"We are no longer colonists," the people said. "We are Americans. The name of our country now is the United States of America."

Benjamin Franklin was now seventy years old. But there was still important work left for him to do. His hair was gray. He wore glasses of a special kind that he had invented. He was rather tired these days and he walked slowly. But his eyes were bright, and his face was kind and happy. Of all the leaders in the United States of America he was one of the most admired.

"We are going to need money and other help," said the Americans. "We must send our wisest men to France to speak for us."

One of the men who was sent to France was Benjamin Franklin. At first France could not decide whether to help the United States. But the French people loved Benjamin Franklin. The King listened to him. Finally, France decided to send aid.

At last the United States of America won its fight for freedom from Great Britain. France was a great help in that struggle. The United States became an independent nation.

Few men of that time did more for our country and the world than did Benjamin Franklin.

Essay Questions: On a sheet of paper answer the following questions:

1. What was one reason why the colonists did *not* like the stamp act?
2. Describe three ways that Benjamin Franklin helped his country.
3. How are the contributions of Benjamin Franklin important to us today?

Check your answers with those found in Appendix B.

Vocabulary Exercise: On a sheet of paper, place the letter of the best answer next to the number for each vocabulary word.

1. declaration
   "It was called the Declaration of Independence."
   a. argument
   b. statement
   c. composition
   d. defense

2. independence
   "That's why the Fourth of July is called Independence Day."
   a. freedom
   b. obligation
   c. compromise
   d. celebration

3. instant
   "The sparks were gone in an instant."
   a. slowly
   b. quickly
   c. generally
   d. completely

4. united

"The name of our country now is the United States of America."

   a. separated
   b. combined
   c. paired
   d. alone

5. prevent

"Wisely and calmly he did his best to prevent war. . . ."

   a. incite
   b. prolong
   c. delay
   d. stop

6. admire

"Of all the leaders . . . he was one of the most admired."

   a. respected
   b. wealthy
   c. forgotten
   d. contented

7. invented

"Benjamin invented the lightning rod."

   a. destroyed
   b. created
   c. sold
   d. perfected

Check your answers with those found in Appendix B.

Time Conversion Chart

Min:Sec	WPM	Min:Sec	WPM	Min:Sec	WPM	Min:Sec	WPM	Min:Sec	WPM
1:00	775	2:30	332	3:50	202	5:10	150	6:30	119
1:20	664	2:40	391	4:00	194	5:20	145	6:40	116
1:30	581	2:50	274	4:10	186	5:30	141	6:50	113
1:40	517	3:00	258	4:20	179	5:40	137	7:00	111
1:50	465	3:10	245	4:30	172	5:50	133		
2:00	423	3:20	233	4:40	166	6:00	129		
2:10	387	3:30	221	4:50	160	6:10	125		
2:20	358	3:40	211	5:00	155	6:20	122		

THE GREEK WAY OF LIFE

The Greeks took these new ideas and began to improve on them.* During the years between 1000 B.C. and 500 B.C., they became civilized. They learned to weave cloth, and to make beautiful vases and bowls. They built houses in towns, and temples to their gods. They learned to build excellent ships, and became as good sailors as the Phoenicians.

Greece with its fine harbors was a good homeland for sailors. The Greeks became traders, also. They planted colonies far to the west: Syracuse on the island of Sicily, and Tarentum on the southern coast of Italy. Still other Greek colonies grew up on the coast of Asia Minor, and became busy trading ports. Many of these settlements grew to be rich and important cities. Locate all of these colonies on the map. They are sometimes called Great Greece, for in each of them was found the Greek way of life.

The Greeks worshiped many gods. They believed that each god or goddess had power over some part of their lives. Apollo was god of the sun, of health, and of music. Artemis was goddess of the moon and of hunting. Athena was goddess of wisdom. There was a god of war, and a god of fire, and many other gods and goddesses. Zeus was the father and ruler of all gods and men.

The Greeks loved to tell stories about their gods. These stories make the gods seem very much like human beings, only more powerful and magnificent. After the Greeks learned to write, they set down hundreds of these stories, which we can still read today.

The Greeks also had stories about their heroes. During the years when they were conquering Greece and settling the islands of the Aegean, they fought many battles. They told tales of these battles and of the daringness of their leaders, and sang songs about their bravery and skill. The blind poet Homer gathered these legends together in two famous books which we still read today. One of them, called the Iliad, tells the story of the Trojan War and the capture of Troy, a city of Asia Minor, by Greek soldiers. The other is called the Odyssey. It tells the adventures of Odysseus, one of the soldier kings returning from the war. Both are full of stirring tales. They are among the greatest poems of all times.

The Greeks had no nation. All Greeks spoke almost the same language, followed the same customs, and worshiped the same gods, but they were not under one government. Mountains divided the land into little enclosed valleys, and kept the groups apart, each where it had settled. In each valley grew a city, surrounded by vineyards, olive trees, and fields of wheat and barley, which supplied the people with food, oil, and wine.

Each of these cities became a separate little state. Each had its own special holidays, its own favorite god, its own trade, its own colonies, and its own government. Some city-states were governed by a king, some by a council, or by a group of wise men. Four important city-states were Sparta, in the southern part of the Peloponnesus; Olympia, in the western part; Corinth, on the narrow isthmus; and Athens, to the east of the isthmus. By 500 B.C. these were strong cities. You can find them on your map of Greece.

The Greeks loved athletic games and contests. Once every four years the city of Olympia invited all Greeks to come to the celebration of a religious festival in honor of Zeus, "father of gods and men." There were contests of skill: running, jumping, wrestling, throwing the spear and the discus. The finest athletes from all over Greece took part. The winners were crowned with olive wreaths and were treated with great honor. The contests were known as the Olympic games. The Olympic games of modern times are named for these games of old Greece.

Often the city-states quarreled bitterly. They sometimes made war upon one another. The Greeks loved their freedom and were always afraid someone might try to take it away. They disliked any state, even any Greek state, which grew richer or more powerful than the others.

*From Your World and Mine, New Edition by Grace S. Dawson, of THE TIEGS-ADAMS SERIES, © Copyright, 1965, 1951, by Ginn and Company (Xerox Corporation). Used with permission.

They feared that a powerful state might suddenly seize their city and make them slaves or demand tax money called *tribute* from them. Sparta and Athens were the strongest of these cities, and were always great rivals.

Sparta was a military city. It was ruled by two kings and a council of older men. The people of Sparta lived almost entirely out of doors, and all the boys were trained as soldiers. At the age of seven they left home to live in special camps. Here all the men, even those who were married, came to eat together. They ate plain food, exercised day after day, and were taught to suffer pain without making a sound. Even today anyone who suffers great pain without complaining is called a Spartan.

The women, too, received athletic training. They took part in the life of their city, and were taught to be strong and brave.

Athens was a very different kind of city. Here, too, a boy started going to school at seven, but he lived at home. He was trained in athletics, but also learned to sing and to play on the lyre, a small harp. He learned the poems which told the legends and history of Greece, as Jason did in our story. When he was eighteen he entered military training, but only for two years. He also prepared himself to become a citizen of Athens. As a citizen he would help govern his city. To prepare himself he joined the older men in the public places and took part in their discussions. They talked of the things that happened in their city, and of their ideas about life. They listened to those who had traveled, or to those who had thought deeply. They were especially fond of talking about the "good life."

The good life meant more things to the people of Athens than to the Spartans. The Athenians wanted more than food and safety and military strength. They wanted beautiful things, and they wanted interesting ideas and thoughts. The Athenians believed it was important to think and talk about all these things.

Athenian women, however, were not free as the women of Sparta. They lived very quietly at home, managing their houses and their slaves, and were seldom seen in public.

Athens was the first democracy. Democracy is a Greek word which means "rule by the people." All free men over thirty who had been born in Athens could vote in the assembly. The assembly met to pass laws and decide public questions. All free men also served in the courts of law and drew lots for public office. Only the highest officials were elected, all the rest were chosen by lot. So almost every citizen had his turn at holding an office. Of course not every man made a good official. But the men of Athens thought this was the best way to divide the honor.

Athens was proud of her democracy and the freedom of her citizens. But there were many who lived in Athens who were not allowed to be citizens. One third of the people of Athens were slaves. A captive taken in war was forced to be the slave of his conqueror. Such captives were bought and sold in the market and were made to do the heavy work of the country. They dragged the stone and marble for buildings or pulled the oars of ships. Household slaves had an easier life. If they had a good education, they taught the children of their master. A slave who was a skillful worker at some art or trade might be paid a little and allowed to buy his freedom.

The women of Athens were not citizens either. They were loved and cared for. But they were not considered the equals of men and took no part in the life of their city. Stranger still, those men who came from other places to live in Athens could not become citizens, no matter how long they lived in the city. The men of Athens would not share their freedom with new friends or with conquered foes, nor even with the women of their own families. Real freedom in Athens belonged to only a small group.

Essay Questions: On a sheet of paper answer the following questions:

1. Who was Zeus?
2. Why was Sparta considered a military city?
3. How does our present-day democracy compare with that of the Greek's early democracy?

Check your answers with those found in Appendix B.

Vocabulary Exercise: On a separate sheet of paper, place the letter of the best answer next to the number for each vocabulary word.

1. improve
   "The Greeks took these new ideas and began to improve them."
   a. change
   b. better
   c. rearrange
   d. ignore

2. excellent
   "They learned to build excellent ships. . . ."
   a. unusual
   b. inferior
   c. fantastic
   d. unique

3. conquering
   ". . . when they were conquering Greece and settling the islands. . . ."
   a. fighting for
   b. ruling
   c. defeating
   d. building up

4. customs
   "All Greeks . . . followed the same customs."
   a. traditions
   b. leaders
   c. religion
   d. laws

5. festival
   ". . . all Greeks came to the celebration of a religious festival. . . ."
   a. service
   b. sacrifice
   c. holiday
   d. activity

6. seize
   ". . . that a powerful state might suddenly seize their city. . . ."
   a. attack
   b. capture
   c. tax
   d. devour

7. complaining

". . . anyone who suffers great pain without complaining is called. . . ."

   a. whining
   b. crying
   c. talking
   d. changing

Check your answers with those found in Appendix B.

Time Conversion Chart

Min:Sec	WPM	Min:Sec	WPM	Min:Sec	WPM	Min:Sec	WPM	Min:Sec	WPM
1:00	848	2:30	339	4:00	212	5:30	154	7:00	121
1:10	727	2:40	318	4:10	204	5:40	150	7:10	118
1:20	636	2:50	299	4:20	196	5:50	145	7:20	116
1:30	565	3:00	283	4:30	188	6:00	141	7:30	113
1:40	509	3:10	268	4:40	182	6:10	137	7:40	111
1:50	462	3:20	254	4:50	175	6:20	134	7:50	108
2:00	424	3:30	242	5:00	170	6:30	130	8:00	106
2:10	391	3:40	231	5:10	164	6:40	127		
2:20	363	3:50	221	5:20	159	6:50	124		

HOW TO READ A ROAD MAP

by Julie Jennings

In this automotive age it is no longer enough that a passenger be simply a passenger; he—or she—must also be a good map reader and navigator.*

Now that superhighways are the way to go, a road map interpreter is as essential to a smooth trip as shock absorbers. Ask any driver whose travelmate has failed to advise him to edge into the correct lane for an upcoming exit. Say the warning comes so late that he would have to make a dangerous twist around two oil tankers and lumber truck to reach the correct lane in time, or he learns he's reached the exit just as he's whizzing past it. It's enough to make a driver want to drop off his traveling companion in the median. It's particularly upsetting if it's 37 miles to the next exit.

To be a good map reader, take along a magnifying glass for viewing the fine print. If you're doing your own trip routing, also take a marking pen or crayon to trace the way. A flashlight will help a nighttime navigator, unless a map light is installed in the car.

Another boost to a navigator's efficiency is an up-to-date road map. Every year, new towns and new miles of highway are added to the USA. The 1973 Rand McNally Road Atlas, for example, shows nearly 1700 more miles of Interstate Highway System than the 1972 edition. So get a recent road map (the date is usually at the top or bottom of the legend, if not on the front cover). You can get road maps free from service stations of major oil companies, your state highway department, the American Automobile Association (members only), and from several national auto insurance companies. Some oil companies mark the locations of their stations on their maps, a handy reference if your're traveling with a credit card. AAA maps also mark in red the communities with AAA-recommended lodging and dining facilities. Another good navigational aid is the strip map often provided as you enter toll expressways.

To translate the language of your road map, first check the legend, which may vary from mapmaker to mapmaker. Examples: the legends of some maps indicate multi-lane expressways by two black lines filled with green for free expressways, red for toll expressways. A solid black line on some maps indicates a paved road, but a black line on others may be only a muddy rut.

Map legends also show you how to spot campgrounds, national and state parks, recreation areas, and historical monuments.

Perhaps the most important symbol of all, for a modern-day navigator, is the symbol for an expressway interchange. It's indicated as a tiny square by most mapmakers. You're a treasure of a travelmate if you can pinpoint the number of the interchange at which you should exit, or the city names or the highway number for that exit. You should know these things in advance, obviously; in fact, it's a good idea to know also the names or numbers marking the two exists just before yours.

Because of the lack of checkpoints along an expressway, there's no other reliable way to guide a confused motorist in unknown territory. Unless you can identify the exits in advance, you may miss your exit when a big truck blocks your view or when you have a momentary lapse of attention.

Another good way to help the driver is to give him a reasonable estimate of the mileage to the correct exit. So learn to figure mileage according to the scale shown on your road map (one inch usually represents 14 to 20 miles).

After you identify the proper exit, you can still blow your navigating task if you direct your driver onto eastbound highway 46 when it should be westbound highway 46. Two separate exits heading different directions often lead from an interchange, so watch for directional signs.

*Used with permission.

If you're in doubt about an exit, take it. You usually can return to the freeway quickly if you made the wrong move. It's better than going 27 miles out of your way if you miss it.

You won't need a compass if you orient yourself to the direction you're heading by turning your map accordingly. If you're headed south, hold it with south at the top. This technique helps to avoid confusion in determining whether a turn should be to the left or to the right.

Once you've safely guided your driver and vehicle to their stopping-off place for the day, another challenge awaits. Folding a road map can lead to all sorts of complications. The secret is that nearly all maps fold like accordions. Hold the open map with the widest part horizontal, and let it accordion-fold as you bring your hand together. If it's a large map, it may require folding first on one or two horizontal creases. Smaller maps usually accordion-fold first, with only one horizontal crease.

When it's your turn to drive, be patient with your map reader. Who knows better than you that his task takes concentration and skill?

Essay Questions: On a sheet of paper answer the following questions:

1. How can a map legend help you read a road map?
2. Why did the author write this article?
3. If you were going on a long trip with your family what should you pack to help you make navigation during the trip easier?

Check your answers with those found in Appendix B.

Vocabulary Exercise: On a sheet of paper, place the letter of the best answer next to the number for each vocabulary word.

1. recent
   ". . . so get a recent road map before leaving. . . ."
   a. new
   b. reliable
   c. expensive
   d. well-marked

2. reference
   ". . . a handy reference if you're traveling with a credit card."
   a. source of money
   b. a repair shop for travelers
   c. a state wide emergency number
   d. place to return to for information

3. blow
   ". . . you can still blow your navigating task. . . ."
   a. explain
   b. correct
   c. fail
   d. complete

4. complications
   "Folding a road map can lead to all sorts of complications. . . ."
   a. puzzles
   b. anger
   c. difficulties
   d. mistakes

5. treasure

"You're a treasure of a travelmate if you. . . ."

a. pleasure to be with
b. worth your weight in gold
c. friend who helps willingly
d. distraction to the driver

6. orient

"You won't need a compass if you orient yourself."

a. determine the direction
b. find the way
c. explain
d. develop

7. reliable

". . . there is no other reliable way of doing this. . . ."

a. interesting
b. trusted
c. avoidable
d. creative

Check your answers with those found in Appendix B.

Time Conversion Chart

Min:Sec	WPM	Min:Sec	WPM	Min:Sec	WPM	Min:Sec	WPM	Min:Sec	WPM
1:00	925	3:00	308	5:00	185	7:00	132	9:00	103
1:10	793	3:10	292	5:10	179	7:10	129	9:10	101
1:20	694	3:20	278	5:20	173	7:20	126	9:20	99
1:30	617	3:30	264	5:30	168	7:30	123		
1:40	555	3:40	252	5:40	163	7:40	121		
1:50	505	3:50	241	5:50	159	7:50	118		
2:00	463	4:00	231	6:00	154	8:00	116		
2:10	427	4:10	222	6:10	150	8:10	113		
2:20	396	4:20	213	6:20	146	8:20	111		
2:30	370	4:30	206	6:30	142	8:30	109		
2:40	347	4:40	198	6:40	139	8:40	107		
2:50	326	4:50	191	6:50	135	8:50	105		

WHAT MAKES FOOD SPOIL?

Why Food Spoils

Have you ever gone to the breadbox to get a piece of bread only to discover that the bread had some spots of blackish or greenish mold on it?* Or have you ever started to drink some milk and found that it did not taste or smell quite right?

In most cases like these, we say the food is spoiled. What causes food to spoil?

One important reason why any fresh foods spoil is that certain microorganisms, or microbes, get into them and grow. Microorganisms are tiny plants and animals that are found all around you—in the air, in the grounds, in the water. They are on your hands and on your clothes. Everything you touch has microbes on it, but you cannot see them because they are so tiny.

Most of the microorganisms in the world around you will not harm you, and many of them are helpful. Some microorganisms help make changes in the ground so that plants grow well in it. Other microorganisms are used to make medicines. Still others are used to make pickles, bread, cheese.

The harmful microbes are those that cause foods to spoil and the ones that cause disease.

Bacteria, molds, and yeasts are some of the microorganisms that are most likely to get into foods and spoil them. Yeasts are sometimes used, though, in food preparation to make bread and rolls.

How do we know that harmful microbes have been at work in our foods and have spoiled them? It may be because of their strange smell or taste. This happens because, as the microbes eat and digest the food, they produce wastes that cause an unpleasant odor or taste. The food may soon become covered with blackish or greenish mold. In the case of yeasts, a scum may form on liquid foods.

Sometimes, however, there may be no signs—either in the taste, smell, or appearance— that would indicate a food has spoiled.

Eating food that contains many harmful microorganisms can cause people to become sick.

How Foods Are Kept from Spoiling

To help keep foods from spoiling, we have to make sure that bacteria, molds, and yeasts do not grow in the foods. These microorganisms will not grow unless they have the things needed to encourage their growth, things like dampness and warmth. Most microbes grow best in warm but not hot places. And they grow very slowly in cold places.

That is why we try to keep foods that spill easily, foods like milk, butter, eggs, meat, fish, and most fruits and vegetables, in a cold place such as a refrigerator or a freezer. Refrigeration slows bacteria growth, while freezing stops it. This keeps the foods from spoiling as quickly as they otherwise would.

Certain foods are especially apt to spoil in the summer if they are left in a warm place. We read fairly often in the newspapers about people who have become sick at picnics from eating foods that had started to spoil because they had not been kept cool. Foods such as custards, cream fillings in cakes and pies, salad dressings, rice, and cornbread stuffings spoil very easily in summer. Such foods should be kept refrigerated until they are to be eaten.

Leftover foods should also be refrigerated to keep them from spoiling. Frozen foods that have been thawed should not be refrozen.

To help keep bacteria out of foods and lessen their chance of spoiling and of making you sick, care must be taken in preparing foods, too. Microorganisms can get into foods by someone's coughing or sneezing on them. Also, touching foods with hands that are dirty or that

---

*From HEALTH AND GROWTH, Grade 4 by Julius B. Richmond, Elenore T. Pounds, Irma B. Fricke, Dieter H. Sussdorf. Copyright © 1974, 1971 Scott, Foresman and Company. Reprinted by permission.

have an open cut or sore on them can spread germs into the food. Storing foods properly is important, too. Foods like sugar and flour should be kept tightly covered to avoid the spread of disease by insects and other pests.

To make sure the foods you eat are safe, the local health department usually requires foodhandlers in public places to have periodic health examinations. Often classes are given by public health workers to teach food-handlers the sanitary way to do things.

Workers from the public health department also check the cleanliness of food sold in grocery stores and in restaurants. Furthermore, dishwashing and table-setting methods are carefully checked to be sure that eating utensils do not have harmful bacteria on them.

Ways of Processing Food to Keep it from Spoiling

Since microorganisms cannot grow in dry places, one common method of keeping food from spoiling is to dry it.

Just think of all the foods at your house that are kept from spoiling because they have been dried—rice, flour, beans, prunes, powdered milk, raisins. Drying foods is a process that has been used over the centuries. Long ago most food was dried by putting it in the sun. Today food factories have special rooms and equipment for the rapid drying of foods.

Salt can help preserve foods, also, And sometimes vinegar and spices are added to give the foods a taste that many people like. This is what is done with pickles and various spiced vegetables and fruits.

Think, too, about the foods that are bought in cans and jars. Sometimes these cans and jars of food are on the shelf for weeks or months before we open them. What has been done to keep the foods in them from spoiling? At the factory the cans or jars of food are cooked at high enough temperatures to kill any microbes that might be in the food. When the cans come out of the cookers, the food in them is sterile, or free from living microbes.

Foods can be frozen, too, and kept in a freezer for a long time without spoiling. What are some frozen foods you have eaten lately?

You learned earlier about the way of preserving foods known as freeze-drying. Fresh foods are quickly frozen and then dried to remove the liquid content. When they are cooked, water is restored, and they have their original fresh flavor. Some foods processed by this freeze-dry method have been kept unrefrigerated for years without spoiling.

Essay Questions: On a sheet of paper answer the following questions:

1. What environment is best for bacteria, mold, and yeast to grow in?
2. How does food spoil?
3. What can you do to help prevent foods from spoiling?

Check your answers with those found in Appendix B.

Vocabulary Exercise: On a sheet of paper, place the letter of the best answer next to the number for each vocabulary word.

1. unpleasant
   ". . . they produce wastes that cause an *unpleasant* odor or taste."
   a. strong
   b. pleasant
   c. acceptable
   d. undesirable

2. scum

"In the case of yeasts, a scum may form on liquid foods."

   a. clean covering
   b. dirty covering
   c. clear covering
   d. thick covering

3. properly

"Storing foods properly is important. . . ."

   a. slowly
   b. quickly
   c. correctly
   d. immediately

4. requires

". . . the local health department usually requires foodhandlers in public places to have periodic health examinations."

   a. suggests
   b. demands
   c. favors
   d. urges

5. processed

"Some foods processed by this freeze-dry method have been kept refrigerated. . . ."

   a. ruined
   b. wasted
   c. passed
   d. treated

6. preserve

"Salt can help preserve food. . . ."

   a. destroy
   b. protect
   c. improve
   d. season

7. restored

"When they are cooked, water is restored. . . ."

   a. add minerals
   b. removed
   c. clean
   d. return

Check your answers with those found in Appendix B.

Time Conversion Chart

Min:Sec	WPM	Min:Sec	WPM	Min:Sec	WPM	Min:Sec	WPM	Min:Sec	WPM
1:00	1010	2:50	356	4:40	216	6:30	155	8:20	121
1:10	866	3:00	337	4:50	209	6:40	151	8:30	119
1:20	758	3:10	319	5:00	202	6:50	148	8:40	117
1:30	673	3:20	303	5:10	195	7:00	144	8:50	114
1:40	606	3:30	289	5:20	189	7:10	141	9:00	112
1:50	551	3:40	275	5:30	184	7:20	138	9:10	110
2:00	505	3:50	263	5:40	178	7:30	135	9:20	108
2:10	466	4:00	253	5:50	173	7:40	132	9:30	106
2:20	433	4:10	242	6:00	168	7:50	129	9:40	104
2:30	404	4:20	233	6:10	164	8:00	126	9:50	103
2:40	379	4:30	224	6:20	159	8:10	124	10:00	101

EUROPEANS ARRIVE IN THE MIDDLE COLONIES

Inquiry: How were settlements in New York, New Jersey, Pennsylvania, and Delaware started?

In 1609, two years after Jamestown was settled, a Dutch ship sailed along the Atlantic coast.* The ship was called the *Half Moon.* Its captain was Henry Hudson. Hudson was an English sailor who had been hired by Dutch merchants to find a passage through America to the Far East. More than a hundred years after Columbus' voyage, Europeans were still looking for a shorter route to the Indies. Hudson did not find a shorter route, but he sailed a mighty river which now bears his name.

Although Hudson did not find what he was sent for, he did explore the land along the Hudson River. He found that the woods were rich in fur-bearing animals. He reported that the Indians were willing to trap these animals and sell them cheaply. When the Dutch merchants learned this, they formed the Dutch West India Company. The company wanted to trade in furs with the Indians and to settle the land explored by Hudson. They sent out the colonists to establish settlements along the Hudson River.

The first Dutch settlers came to America in 1623. The governor of their colony, Peter Minuit, bought the island of Manhattan from the Indians. The island cost Minuit $24 worth of colored beads and trinkets. A fort and a village were built on the island, which then became known as New Amsterdam. Some of the Dutch went up the Hudson River and built Fort Orange, where the city of Albany now stands. Some moved near the Connecticut River. Still others settled near the Delaware River. These four settlements made up the colony of New Netherlands.

To encourage more people to come to the colony, the Dutch West India Company promised to give land along the Hudson River to any person who would bring fifty people to the colony. These people were to settle on the land. The landowners became known as "patroons."

One of the most famous governors of New Netherlands was Peter Stuyvesant. He was an old soldier who had lost a leg in the wars. He was not well-liked because his rule was strict.

Sweden is a small country in Northern Europe. In 1638, Swedish settlers built a fort at what is now Wilmington, Delaware. The fort was named Christina, in honor of the Swedish queen. The Swedes did not know that the Dutch had already settled in Delaware. More settlers arrived and the colony was called New Sweden. The earlier Dutch settlers called for help. In 1655, Peter Stuyvesant marched south with his soldiers. The Swedish colony was captured and brought under Dutch rule.

Trouble developed between the Dutch and the English. England claimed all the land along the eastern coast because of the voyages of John Cabot. The quarrel grew steadily worse. In 1664, war broke out between the two countries. An English fleet sailed into the harbor of New Amsterdam and demanded the surrender of the Dutch. Stuyvesant wanted to fight but the Dutch settlers would not support him. New Netherlands became an English colony.

The King of England turned the colony over to his brother, the Duke of York. The name was changed to New York in honor of the new ruler. At the same time, England had gained land across the Hudson River. The Dutch and Swedes had settled there but it was now English territory. The Duke of York gave this land to two English noblemen who named their colony New Jersey.

When the Dutch were losing New Amsterdam to the English, there lived in England a remarkable young man by the name of William Penn. He had become a member of a religious group called the Society of Friends, or Quakers. The religious practices of the Quakers were simple. When they met to worship God, there was no preacher. Everyone was free to speak. They believed all men were equal before God. They refused to take off their hats for anyone.

*Melvin Schwartz and John R. O'Connor, THE NEW EXPLORING AMERICAN HISTORY, p. 119, copyright © 1981 Globe Book Company, Inc. Used by permission.

They did not swear loyalty to the king. They hated war. They thought it was wrong to keep slaves. Because of their beliefs, the Quakers were forbidden to preach in England. If they disobeyed the king, they were put in prison or fined heavily. William Penn at one time went to jail for his religious beliefs.

Penn had a rich and famous father, Admiral Penn. The king owed a large sum of money to the admiral. Penn tried to collect the money after his father's death, but he did not succeed. William suggested that the king give him a grant of land in America in return for the debt. Penn wanted the land for the Quakers so they could be free to worship as they wished. The king agreed. The land given to Penn became known as Pennsylvania (Penn's Woods).

William Penn came to Pennsylvania in 1682. Although he had a charter giving him the land, he paid the Indians for it. He wanted to live in peace and friendship with the Indians. His peace treaty with the Indians was never broken during his lifetime. For the capital of his colony, he chose the place where the city of Philadelphia now stands. Philadelphia means "brotherly love."

Penn opened his colony to others besides Quakers. He sent out notices to England, Ireland, Scotland, and Germany, promising freedom of worship and cheap land to all who would come to Pennsylvania. Thousands came. They were allowed to buy land for as little as a penny an acre. They took part in the government of the colony. They worshiped in their own manner. They built towns, raised crops and were happy and prosperous. Pennsylvania became one of the most successful of all the English colonies. It became known as a place where people of all races and religious beliefs were treated equally.

The little colony which the Swedes had started became known as Delaware. The English gained this colony after their war with the Dutch. The Duke of York gave it to William Penn to govern. In 1704, it became a separate colony.

Essay Questions: On a sheet of paper answer the following questions:

1. How did William Penn get his land in the middle colonies?
2. What was the difference between the Quakers and other religious groups in the colonies?
3. Why was the Dutch West India colony founded?

Check your answers with those found in Appendix B.

Vocabulary Exercise: On a sheet of paper, place the letter of the best answer next to the number for each vocabulary word.

1. encourage
   "To encourage more people to come to the colony, the Dutch West India Company promised to give land. . . ."

   a. prevent
   b. coax
   c. stop
   d. tell
2. strict
   "He was not well-liked because his rule was strict."

   a. complete
   b. unfair
   c. cruel
   d. harsh

3. quarrel
"The quarrel grew steadily worse."

a. argument
b. situation
c. trouble
d. problem

4. surrender
". . . and demanded the surrender of the Dutch."

a. winning
b. land
c. giving up
d. victory

5. debt
"William suggested that the king give him a grant of land in America in return for the debt."

a. money due
b. amount paid
c. gold
d. work

6. establish
"They sent out colonists to establish settlements along the Hudson River."

a. work
b. find
c. start
d. show

7. honor
"The name was changed to New York in honor of the new ruler."

a. memory
b. concern
c. kindness
d. respect

Check your answers with those found in Appendix B.

Time Conversion Chart

Min:Sec	WPM	Min:Sec	WPM	Min:Sec	WPM	Min:Sec	WPM	Min:Sec	WPM
1:00	794	2:30	317	4:00	198	5:30	144	7:00	113
1:10	680	2:40	298	4:10	190	5:40	140	7:10	110
1:20	595	2:50	280	4:20	183	5:50	136	7:20	108
1:30	529	3:00	265	4:30	176	6:00	132	7:30	106
1:40	476	3:10	250	4:40	170	6:10	128	7:40	103
1:50	433	3:20	238	4:50	164	6:20	125	7:50	101
2:00	397	3:30	227	5:00	158	6:30	122	8:00	99
2:10	366	3:40	216	5:10	154	6:40	119		
2:20	340	3:50	207	5:20	419	6:50	116		

THE CAMEL'S SECRET

The camel has long intrigued poet and scientist alike.* Rudyard Kipling wondered how it got its hump. Robert Browning noted its "reserve of scanty water." And the Roman naturalist Pliny the Elder seems to have been the first to liken the camel's stomach to a water tank. But contrary to ancient lore and still popular myth, the ship of the desert is able to survive without drinking for days and even weeks in scorching heat for an entirely different reason. The camel's hump is just a lump of fatty tissue that is consumed when food is scarce. And the beast does not store extra water in its belly or elsewhere. The camel's secret is simply conservation.

Scientists have known since the mid-1950s that the one-humped *Camelus dromedarius* is an animal dedicated to preserving every drop of water in its body tissues. It does so in several ways. Most important, its large, well-insulated body takes a long time to heat up, and when the water supply runs short it can withstand a substantial rise in body temperature; both characteristics reduce the need for perspiration and help keep the loss of water to a minimum. The camel also has kidneys that can retain water, and body tissues that can tolerate both dehydration and the sudden gain of water when the camel quenches its thirst.

Now scientists have discovered that the camel has another important conservation system, one that saves water by removing moisture from air that is being exhaled. The key element in this system is the camel's prodigious nose.

When an ordinary animal breathes out, its body loses water; the exhaled air, at body temperature, is saturated with water vapor picked up from the lungs. But camels are not ordinary. Four years ago, in Kenya, physiologist Knut Schmidt-Nielsen, of Duke University, learned that the camel could exhale air that was cooler than its body temperature. That ability reduces by 45 percent the amount of water usually lost through respiration, because cool air holds less water vapor than hot air.

In the latest dromedary discovery, Schmidt-Nielsen and zoologist Amiram Shkolnik, of Tel Aviv University, have found that the camel's nose carries this effort one step further: it absorbs a good part of the moisture in the outgoing air. They conducted their tests on two female dromedaries borrowed from children's zoos. ("We wanted the tamest animals we could find," explained Shkolnik. "If those big animals don't cooperate, there is nothing you can do with them.") The camels were kept for 16 days in a corral, without shade or shelter, at a kibbutz on the arid shore of the Dead Sea. Mid-July temperatures there, a quarter of a mile below sea level, soared above 104 degrees Fahrenheit during the day.

The animals were fed dry hay and a few green dates, but no liquids. A sensor in the nostrils monitored temperature and humidity changes in the air they breathed. As the camels began to dehydrate and lose weight, their exhaled air became cooler and drier; at night it dropped 18 degrees below body temperature, and was only 70 to 75 per cent saturated. Said Shkolnik: "Exhaling unsaturated air had never before been described in any animal. We had to discover how the camel did it."

An examination of the nasal passages disclosed the answer. Transverse sections cut through the nasal regions of camel skulls revealed a series of involuted air passages. The folds, covered by mucous membrane, provide a surface area of more than 155 square inches (air passages in a human nose have less than two).

The membrane is coated with a water-absorbent substance. As wet, warm air from the lungs travels through the passages, the membrane removes moisture and heat. Inhaled air is moisturized by the membrane, which is cooled and dried in the process so that during the next

*Carol Johmann, *Discover* Magazine, © 1980 Time Inc.

breathing cycle it can again cool and desaturate exhaled air. The overall saving in water, between cooling and drying: 68 per cent of the water usually lost through respiration. Thus does the camel's outwardly magnificent, inwardly marvelous nose contribute nobly to the dromedary's defiance of the desert.

Essay Questions: On a sheet of paper answer the following questions:

1. What happened when two scientists kept two camels in the heat without water for 16 days?
2. How does the camel practice water conservation?
3. Why are most animals and humans more thirsty on hot days than on cooler days?

Check your answers with those found in Appendix B.

Vocabulary Exercise: On a sheet of paper, place the letter of the best answer next to the number for each vocabulary word.

1. scorching
   ". . . is able to survive without drinking water for days and even weeks in scorching heat. . . ."
   a. burning
   b. trying
   c. withering
   d. ongoing

2. prodigious
   "The key element in this system is the camel's prodigious nose."
   a. small
   b. curved
   c. marvelous
   d. protruding

3. quenches
   "The camel also has kidneys that can retain water . . . and the sudden gain of water when the camel quenches its thirst."
   a. interrupts
   b. satisfies
   c. increases
   d. teases

4. conservation
   "The camel's secret is simply conservation."
   a. stubborness
   b. stoutness
   c. saving
   d. hardiness

5. intrigued
   "The camel has long intrigued poet and scientist alike."
   a. puzzled
   b. pestered
   c. threatened
   d. fascinated

6. consumed

"The camel's hump is just a lump of fatty tissue that is consumed when food is scarce."

    a. to change form

    b. to make more

    c. to use up

    d. to reconstitute

7. tolerate

". . . and body tissues that can tolerate both dehydration and the sudden gain of water. . . ."

    a. to bear

    b. to eliminate

    c. to conserve

    d. to torment

Check your answers with those found in Appendix B.

Time Conversion Chart

Min:Sec	WPM	Min:Sec	WPM	Min:Sec	WPM	Min:Sec	WPM	Min:Sec	WPM
1:00	830	2:30	332	4:00	207	5:30	151	7:00	118
1:10	711	2:40	311	4:10	199	5:40	146	7:10	116
1:20	622	2:50	293	4:20	191	5:50	142	7:20	113
1:30	553	3:00	277	4:30	184	6:00	138	7:30	110
1:40	498	3:10	262	4:40	178	6:10	134	7:40	108
1:50	452	3:20	249	4:50	172	6:20	131	7:50	106
2:00	415	3:30	237	5:00	166	6:30	127	8:00	103
2:10	383	3:40	226	5:10	160	6:40	124		
2:20	355	3:50	216	5:20	155	6:50	121		

ENERGY FOR THE FUTURE

Energy lies everywhere around us but where does energy come from: The energy we use comes from the sun, except for nuclear energy.* The sun gives off tremendous heat and light, and some of the sun's rays strike the earth. They fall on green plants that use the sun's energy to grow.

Then animals eat the green plants. The energy changes again, this time to animal tissues. When predators eat meat, energy goes from one animal to the other. When a dead animal decays, energy escapes as heat, or is stored in the soil.

Energy from the sun also goes into wood for storage. Burn the wood for fuel, and you release its energy as heat. Millions of years ago energy from plants and animals went into the ground as coal, oil, and natural gas.

How we live in the future will depend on how carefully we use the stored energy that is left, and whether we find new sources of energy to do our work.

In ancient times strange-looking giant ferns and primitive trees grew in the hot steamy swamps. Fish and amphibians swam in warm shallow waters. There were giant insects, but there were no birds singing 300 million years ago, and no mammals calling.

Beneath the hot sun the swamp forests grew steadily. Then they died and fell into the swamp to rot. More plants grew on top of them. These also died and fell down to rot. This went on for thousands of years. The layer of rotting plants and animals built up thicker and thicker. The rotting plants formed peat. This was the first step toward one of our most important sources of energy.

Beneath the broad swamps the earth shifted. Parts of it sank. Then water rushed in to fill the low places. This water carried mud and sand that built up where the swamps had been. The weight of the water and mud pressed down on the peat. Time passed and the pressure continued until the peat hardened into rock. This rock was coal. The energy the plants gathered from the sun over thousands of years remained in the coal.

The United States has one-fifth of the world's coal. It leads the world in coal production.

Many products, including perfume and synthetic rubber, can be made from coal. The *big* job we give to coal is to fuel our electric generating plants.

Coal can be taken by stripping off the soil above it when the coal lies close to the surface. Strip mining tears up the land. Coal buried deeper in the earth can be reached by deep mining. Miners may work a mile or more underground. There they operate big coal-cutting machines, then load the coal onto cars or conveyor belts that move it up to the surface.

Next, the coal must be transported where it is needed to burn in power plants. Mining and moving coal takes large amounts of energy. Much coal is hauled on trains, barges, and trucks. Coal can also be moved by crushing it into a powder, then mixing it with water to make a black slurry that can be pumped through giant pipes.

Sometimes power plants are built near the coal mines so the coal does not have to be moved far. High power transmission lines stretched over the countryside carry the electric power to distant cities.

People have known about oil for hundreds of years. North American Indians used this fossil fuel long before the settlers came. Some of the black liquid seeped from the ground. More was taken from wells dug with stone tools. The Indians who found oil sometimes used it for fuel instead of wood. They used it as medicine, too.

In the early 1850s, a businessman decided that oil might be a product he could sell. This led to the first modern oil well.

That first well was 69 1/2 feet deep; oil rose partway to the surface. It was pumped the rest of the way. Then it sold for $20 a barrel.

*Reprinted by permission of the author and *Boy's Life*.

Soon refineries were built. More oil wells were drilled. Horse-drawn wagons, river barges, and railroads carried the oil. Beginning in 1865, pipelines were built for moving oil from the oil fields to the refineries.

The demand for oil grew quickly. New oil fields were found in several states. Most of this oil was refined into kerosene to use in lamps. About the time electric lights took the place of kerosene lamps, the automobile came along. Oil production and the automobile—a new use for fuel—grew together. Better engines were built. Meanwhile, gasoline was improving.

Today petroleum products keep our cars, trucks, boats, airplanes, and trains going. Because of the energy in oil we have built highways for our millions of automobiles and trucks. We have also built giant airports.

In the United States our use of energy grew and grew. Our demands for more energy continue to grow. We use a third of all the energy produced in the world. Yet, we have only one-sixth of the world's people.

We must buy much of the oil we use from other countries to get enough. The long distance the oil is moved increases the price. It also puts us at the mercy of the countries that sell us oil. They raise the prices of oil, and we pay it. They can cut off oil supplies whenever they want to.

This keeps us looking for new oil fields in the United States. One of the biggest ones was found in 1968, in northern Alaska. The cost of drilling for this oil in Arctic weather and then moving it to market, however, is high.

We have not yet found all the oil. The search for more goes on all the time. One of the places now being searched is deep in the earth beneath the oceans.

Even when we use oil, it brings problems. It is not a clean source of energy. It causes air pollution when we burn its products in our vehicles and furnaces.

Oil wells sometimes erupt and the oil escapes. Oil tankers wreck and spill more oil. Oil pipelines spring leaks. When spilled oil gets into lakes, rivers, or the ocean, it can kill fish, birds, and other animals. It turns beaches black and sticky.

We use more oil than we should. The fact is that the world's supply of oil is limited, and we will someday run out of oil. The earth's oil took millions of years to form. But people may use it up within 200 years.

Essay Questions: On a sheet of paper answer the following questions:

1. How much of the world's coal is found in the U.S.?
2. How is coal formed?
3. What are some potential problems we face in the future with oil?

Check your answers with those found in Appendix B.

Vocabulary Exercise: On a sheet of paper, place the letter of the best answer next to the number for each vocabulary word.

1. tremendous
   "The sun gives off tremendous heat and light."
   a. ample
   b. trivial
   c. sufficient
   d. immense

2. ancient

"In ancient times strange-looking giant ferns grew. . . ."

   a. very old
   b. novel
   c. recent
   d. modern

3. synthetic

"Many products, including perfume and synthetic rubber can be made from coal."

   a. natural
   b. spontaneous
   c. man-made
   d. simple

4. barges

"Much coal is hauled on trains, barges, and trucks."

   a. wagons
   b. boats
   c. trailers
   d. kegs

5. pollution

"It causes air *pollution* when we burn its products in our vehicles and furnaces."

   a. purification
   b. contamination
   c. filtration
   d. distillation

6. primitive

"In ancient times strange-looking giant ferns and primitive trees grew. . . ."

   a. simple
   b. small
   c. complex
   d. green

7. shifted

"Beneath the broad swamps the earth shifted."

   a. leveled
   b. hardened
   c. flattened
   d. moved

Check your answers with those found in Appendix B.

Time Conversion Chart

Min:Sec	WPM	Min:Sec	WPM	Min:Sec	WPM	Min:Sec	WPM	Min:Sec	WPM
1:00	1050	2:50	370	4:40	225	6:30	161	8:20	126
1:10	900	3:00	350	4:50	217	6:40	157	8:30	123
1:20	787	3:10	331	5:00	210	6:50	154	8:40	121
1:30	700	3:20	315	5:10	203	7:00	150	8:50	119
1:40	630	3:30	300	5:20	197	7:10	146	9:00	116
1:50	572	3:40	286	5:30	191	7:20	143	9:10	114
2:00	525	3:50	274	5:40	185	7:30	140	9:20	112
2:10	484	4:00	262	5:50	180	7:40	137	9:30	110
2:20	450	4:10	252	6:00	175	7:50	134	9:40	109
2:30	420	4:20	242	6:10	170	8:00	131	9:50	106
2:40	394	4:30	233	6:20	166	8:10	128	10:00	105

THE CALIFORNIA GOLD RUSH
Ralph K. Andrist

Whenever the prospectors made a rich strike, there were certain other enterprising men not far behind them.* In no time at all a merchant would arrive and set up a crude store, ready to sell anything from shovels and shirts to tobacco and liniment. Another early arrival would be saloon keeper with his kegs of whiskey and rum. Soon a hotel would be thrown together, a professional gambler would arrive and set up his table, and very shortly, if the gold deposits held out, the camp would become a small city, bustling with business as it served miners who wanted a good many things and had the gold dust to pay for them.

A mining camp was not the place for a poor man. Every miner who ever kept a diary or wrote a letter home commented on the fantastically high prices. One man wrote that he had paid $11 for a jar of pickles and two sweet potatoes, while for one needle and two spools of thread he had to spend $7.50. The price of flour rose as high as $800 a barrel, molasses and vinegar $1 for a 1½-pint bottle, onions up to $2 each, eggs $3 each. And though these prices seem high to us today, they were proportionately even higher in 1849 when a dollar bought much more than it does today.

There was good reason for high prices. Almost everything had to be shipped all the way around Cape Horn from the East to San Francisco, and then carried to the gold fields by boat, wagon, muleback, and sometimes even by human power. Then, of course, the merchants made sure there was a big profit for themselves. Much more money was made in California by the average merchant then was earned by most of the miners panning for gold. But sometimes the greed of a merchant would go too far even for the miners. An old record from Bidwell's Bar says that "Last week a meeting of miners was called to take into consideration the action of a merchant who had been selling Dr. Stover's California Salve for butter."

The hotels were the busiest places in town. Many of them also contained a barroom and a gambling room. Dame Shirley's impressions of the Empire Hotel in Rich Bar, with its strange combination of crudity and elegance, have already been described. The Empire, however, was considerably better than the average; much more typical was a hotel in Sonora of which an account remains. Although the best in town, it was only a one-story structure, built mainly of saplings covered with canvas. The floors were dirt, and one undivided room served as dining room, parlor, and bedroom. There were tables and benches in the center, while along the walls were five-decker bunks built of crude posts and crosspieces fastened with rawhide.

For bedding there was a small straw mattress two feet wide, a straw-stuffed pillow without any casing, and one blanket. "When we creep into one of these nests," a miner wrote, "it is optional with us whether we unboot and uncoat ourselves, but it would be looked upon as an act of ill-breeding to go to bed with one's hat on."

Although such a building was called a hotel, it was really a crude boarding house whose tenants were miners from the nearby diggings. They paid outrageous prices for food and lodging.

John Forthwick has described a meal he had at the United States Hotel while passing through Spanish Bar one day. With sixty or seventy other miners he waited in the saloon until the doors to the adjoining dining room were thrown open; then there was a tremendous rush for places at the benches set on each side of two long tables loaded with ample quantities of roast beef, potatoes, beans, pickles, and salt pork. Not everyone made it, and about twenty unsuccessful men came back into the saloon looking a little sheepish, while from inside there arose a loud clatter of silverware against plates. In an unbelievable short time men began coming out again, many still chewing their last mouthful or picking their teeth with bowie knives.

Then the dining room doors were closed so that the tables could be reset. By the time they were opened again, more miners had arrived, and the same wild rush occurred. Borthwick stationed himself so he could follow in the wake of a broad-shouldered Kentuckian. Once inside, he dashed for a position in front of a large roast beef on a table, and without wasting time trying to sit down, he snatched up a knife and fork and thrust them into the meat. Then, with this for an anchor, he worked his elbows until he had enough room to sit down, while those who had missed getting places this time went back to the saloon to wait for the third table. Borthwick says the diners were all perfectly polite and would pass anything if asked, but they did it with one hand and kept on eating with the other. Their only aim seemed to be to finish as soon as possible and get out of the dining room.

Saloons in the camps did a rushing business, especially at the end of the week, but drunkenness was infrequent. Some men, unable to bear up under the hardships and disappointments of a miner's life, took refuge in drink; but for most the saloon was a place to drop in of an evening and discuss events with friends over a couple of drinks before going to bed.

Strange as it may seem, a saloon owner liked to hire bartenders with broad fingers and thumbs. The price for a drink everywhere in the mines was a pinch of gold dust. The miner brought out his leather pouch, and the bartender took as much gold dust as he could hold between thumb and forefinger. The bigger his fingers, the larger the profit.

A story from Shaw's Flat tells of a bartender who found a way to increase his own income. Whenever he took a pinch of gold in payment for a drink, he managed to spill a few grains on the bar. Not much. Not enough for most miners to pay any attention to; but in an evening it could amount to quite a bit. Each time he wiped the bar he swept the bits of gold behind it, and every once in a while he stepped out the back door to get the bottoms of his boots covered with mud from a spring a few feet away. Then, as he worked, he carefully stepped on every bit of space behind the bar so that all the spilled gold was picked up by sticky mud. After finishing work, he panned out the mud from his boots. It is said that he made about $30 this way every night except on weekends, when his profit was almost $100.

In the early days of the gold rush, a miner's diversions were limited. If he did not want to go to a saloon or to part with his gold by gambling, he had little to do in his spare time. There was an occasional fight between a live bear and a bull, and sometimes there was a horse race where the ground was level enough. As women were a rarity in the diggings, half of the men might tie a bandanna around their arms and be the "ladies" for an evening of dancing. No one thought it strange to see these bearded "ladies" in heavy boots tripping seriously with their partners through the steps of the polka.

But conditions were changing rapidly in California in the early 1850s, and within three or four years after the forty-niners came, more and more amusements were made available to the miners. As crude trails became roads over which stagecoaches could drive, professional entertainers came to the mining towns in the canyons. Before long, every well-established camp with any sort of pride in itself had a theater, singers, variety acts, and theatrical troupes. Even an occasional circus strove for the patronage of the men in the mines.

The miners were enthusiastic when they liked something, but otherwise they were a difficult audience. Lola Montex, who had become famous because of her beauty and her gaudy career rather than because of her talent, drew tremendous audiences in San Francisco; but when she danced at the gold camps the miners were so bored with her that she had to give up her tour. On the other hand, the miners loved Caroline and William Chapman, a brother-and-sister team who came to the camps in 1852 and 1853. They acted in plays, or danced, sang, or clowned as the mood struck them, and their delighted audiences threw coins and pouches of gold dust on stage.

The actor Edwin Booth, brother of the man who killed Lincoln, made several trips through the mining camps between 1852 and 1855, usually playing Shakespearean roles to appreciative crowds of miners. But on one trip, fires broke out in Hangtown, Georgetown, Diamond Springs, Nevada City, and Grass Valley while the theatrical group was in each camp, and the miners began to suspect that the players were either jinxed or had a firebug amongst them. At their next scheduled stop, Booth and his fellows were firmly told to keep moving.

95

Essay Questions: On a sheet of paper answer the following questions:

1. Why were the prices so high in mining towns?
2. How did the gold rush affect California?
3. If oil were discovered today in your town, how would it affect you and your town?

Check your answers with those found in Appendix B.

Vocabulary Exercise: On a sheet of paper, place the letter of the best answer next to the number for each vocabulary word.

1. crude
   "As crude trails became roads the miners. . . ."

   a. rough
   b. straight
   c. dangerous
   d. old

2. sheepish
   ". . . unsuccessful men came back looking a little sheepish. . . . "

   a. surprised
   b. delighted
   c. embarrassed
   d. frightened

3. adjoining
   ". . . the doors to the adjoining dining room were open. . . ."

   a. noisy
   b. expensive
   c. interior
   d. connecting

4. infrequent
   ". . . the saloon did a rushing business but drunkenness was infrequent."

   a. common
   b. expensive
   c. illegal
   d. rare

5. diversions
   "In the early days a miner's diversions were limited."

   a. friends
   b. amusements
   c. funds
   d. organizations

6. rarity
   "As women were a rarity in the diggings. . . ."

   a. different
   b. unusual
   c. plentiful
   d. not present

7. tremendous

"Lola Montex—drew tremendous audiences in San Francisco."

a. small
b. large
c. average
d. medium

Check your answers with those found in Appendix B.

Time Conversion Chart

Min:Sec	WPM	Min:Sec	WPM	Min:Sec	WPM	Min:Sec	WPM	Min:Sec	WPM
1:00	1326	2:20	568	3:40	368	5:00	274	6:20	215
1:10	1136	2:30	530	3:50	361	5:10	265	6:30	209
1:20	994	2:40	497	4:00	345	5:20	256	6:40	204
1:30	884	2:50	468	4:10	331	5:30	248	6:50	199
1:40	796	3:00	442	4:20	318	5:40	241	7:00	194
1:50	723	3:10	418	4:30	306	5:50	234		
2:00	663	3:20	399	4:40	295	6:00	227		
2:10	612	3:30	379	4:50	284	6:10	221		

TAKING THE EARTH'S PULSE

An earthquake is a trembling of the ground.* Most earthquakes are barely noticeable, but some are violent and destructive. The ground can break apart during a violent earthquake, leaving gaping trenches, the remains of demolished buildings, disrupted roadways, displaced railroad tracks, and dangling power lines.

The point at which the first release of the energy that causes an earthquake occurs is called the "earthquake focus." The focus generally lies below the surface. The point on the Earth's surface directly above the focus is referred to as the "epicenter." Scientists describe the location of an earthquake focus by giving the geographic position of its epicenter and its depth.

How is the energy of an earthquake transmitted from the focus to other parts of the Earth? As with any release of energy, vibrations or disturbances spread outward from the focus. The vibrations that go out from an earthquake focus are called "seismic waves," after the Greek word for earthquake. The seismic waves spread out in all directions from the focus, just as sound waves spread out in all directions when a gun is fired.

Seismic waves are the shakers and wreckers that accompany the release of energy at the focus. There are two general types of seismic waves produced by earthquakes: surface waves and body waves.

Surface waves are so named because they travel along the Earth's surface. They produce most of the destruction because they actually make the ground roll. Surface waves are usually stronger than body waves.

The seismic vibrations called "body waves" are sometimes referred to as "preliminary waves" since they arrive before the surface or rolling waves. There are, however, two different and distinct types of body waves. The first is classified as a "compression wave," while the second type is said to be a "shear wave."

The compression waves produced by an earthquake travel at great speeds. They ordinarily are the first signals indicating that an earthquake has occurred. Since they are the first to arrive, compression waves are referred to as the "primary waves," or "P" waves.

A P wave arrives at the surface like a hammerblow. The blow is the result of energy released deep within the Earth. The blow of a P wave travels in the same way that a bump from a locomotive on one freight car travels all the way through a long train.

P waves—like sound waves—move through both liquid and solids by compressing the material directly ahead of them. Each compressed particle, in turn, springs back to its original position as the energy moves on. This event—compression of a particle to its springback— is called a "cycle." The time within which such a cycle is completed is referred to as the wave's "period."

The P wave is the swiftest seismic wave. Its speed, however, varies with the material through which it passes. P-wave velocity in the crust of the Earth usually is less than four miles per second, or 14,000 miles per hour. But just below the crust in the mantle, the speed of a P wave jumps to five miles per second, or 18,000 miles per hour. As a P wave passes deep into the Earth and moves below the mantle through the core, its speed increases to seven miles per second. Thus, it travels through the Earth's core at more than 25,000 miles per hour.

When a P wave strikes an object embedded in the ground, it produces a series of sharp pushes and pulls. These pushes and pulls are in a direction parallel to the wave path. The second type of body wave, on the other hand, produces a shearing effect or a side-to-side shaking of an object embedded in the ground.

*Excerpt from EARTHQUAKE by John G. Navarra. Copyright © 1980 by John Gabriel Navarra. Reprinted by permission of Doubleday & Company, Inc.

The shear waves produced by an earthquake are referred to as "secondary waves," or S waves. One reason for the shear waves to be called secondary is that they ordinarily reach the surface after the P waves. The shear, or S waves displace an object at right angles to their direction of travel and are thus sometimes called "transverse waves."

The S wave must have a rigid medium through which to move. These transverse or shear waves do not travel below the mantle. The outer portion of the Earth's core, which is just below the mantle, is liquid, and S waves cannot travel through it.

Let's stop for a moment and put all this information together. The first signal you get that an earthquake has occurred will often be a sharp thud. The thud, or hammerblow, indicates the arrival of the compression, or P waves. Then the P waves are followed by the shear, or S waves. With the arrival of S waves, objects begin to shake from side to side. Then, when the surface waves arrive, the ground begins to roll.

The vibrations produced by earthquakes are recorded and measured by instruments called seismographs. A variety of different seismographs have been designed because seismic waves have a wide range of periods. Remember, the period of a seismic wave is nothing more than the time within which it completes its cycle. Some waves generated at a focus can have periods that are extremely long. Others have periods of less than a tenth of a second.

Scientists must use different seismographs to record the different waves. Some seismographs are sensitive to short-period waves and others are sensitive to long-period waves.

The general principle of the seismograph is rather simple. You can see how it operates by trying this: Place a half dollar on a scratch pad held horizontally in your hand. Move the pad suddenly forward and then back. Now, just as suddenly, move the pad sideways and then back. The half dollar tends to remain in one place while the scratch pad slips about under it. A seismograph is nothing more than an instrument that has a weight supported clear of the ground and freely suspended.

When P, S, and surface waves travel through the Earth to a seismograph, they shake the supports on which the weight hangs. But the weight, because of its inertia, tends to remain steady in one place. A recording needle, or pen, attached to the weight is used to trace a graph on a revolving drum that is attached to the supports of the apparatus. In other words, body waves (P and S) and the surface waves shake the supports of the seismograph. In turn, the supports shake the revolving drum and the paper on it. Everything shakes except the steady mass of the weight and the pen attached to it. In this way, a pen writes a record of the vibrations.

The zigzag line made by the pen of a seismograph is called a *seismogram*. The seisomogram is marked with a time scale. Each unit on the time scale is one minute. The waves recorded by the seismograph prior to the arrival of the P-wave train represent the background vibration that exists at Florissant. This is a continuous record of exceedingly small waves. The small waves are known as *microseisms*. The microseisms are made by disturbances other than earthquakes.

Remember, P and S waves leave the earthquake focus at the same instant. They travel outward in all directions. The fast-moving P waves reach the seismograph first. Then, some time later, the slower-moving S waves arrive. The delay in arrival time is proportional to the distance traveled by the waves. In other words, the farther away the center, or focus, of the earthquake shock is, the longer is the spread of time between the arrival of the P and the S waves.

The data recorded in a seismograph allow the scientists to describe the earthquake. The recorded heights, or amplitudes, of the P,S, and surface waves, for example, indicate the amount of energy released. By combining data from selected seismograph stations, the epicenter and the focal depth of an earthquake can be located.

In the case of a violent dislocation that produces a severe earthquake, the energy is released in one large wrench followed by smaller tremors. The tremors are referred to as "aftershocks." The aftershocks are produced by the continuing collapse and movement of crustal blocks. Sometimes the violent wrench is preceded by small structural failures that produce foreshocks. The foreshocks are really small tremors.

News about an earthquake nearly always causes a person to ask: What happened to people in the area? Were many buildings destroyed? How severe was the quake? Most reports of such an event include a statement that attempts to rank the earthquake.

At the present time, two scales are used to describe the severity of an earthquake: the Richter scale and the modified Mercalli scale. The Richter and Mercalli scales are completely separate in intent.

The Richter scale measures an earthquake in terms of its energy or magnitude at the moment when it begins. Magnitude is expressed as a number on the Richter scale. The number is derived from the amplitude of the recorded seismic waves. Thus, the Richter scale is based on instrument records.

Essay Questions: On a sheet of paper answer the following questions:

1. What are the two general types of seismic waves produced by earthquakes?
2. What is an earthquake?
3. Why is the recorded data on earthquakes important to scientists?

Check your answers with those found in Appendix B.

Vocabulary Exercise: On a sheet of paper, place the letter of the best answer next to the number for each vocabulary word.

1. trembling
   "An earthquake is a *trembling* of the ground."
   a. eruption
   b. shaking
   c. rolling
   d. displacement

2. violent
   "Most earthquakes are barely noticeable, but some are *violent* and destructive.
   a. strong
   b. frequent
   c. excessive
   d. loud

3. transmitted
   "How is the energy of an earthquake *transmitted* from the focus to other parts of the earth?"
   a. detected
   b. removed
   c. recorded
   d. sent

4. distinct
   "There are two different and *distinct* types of body waves."
   a. usual
   b. remote
   c. unusual
   d. separate

5. compressing

"P waves move through both liquids and solids by *compressing* the material directly ahead of them."

   a. stretching out
   b. squeezing together
   c. folding up
   d. spreading out

6. velocity

"P-wave *velocity* in the crust of the earth usually is less than four miles per second."

   a. height
   b. distance
   c. speed
   d. measurement

7. suspended

"A seismograph is nothing more than an instrument that has a weight supported clear of the ground and freely *suspended*."

   a. stopped
   b. hung
   c. removed
   d. stretched

Check your answers with those found in Appendix B.

Time Conversion Chart

Min:Sec	WPM	Min:Sec	WPM	Min:Sec	WPM	Min:Sec	WPM	Min:Sec	WPM
1:00	1326	3:10	418	5:20	248	7:30	176	9:40	137
1:10	1136	3:20	398	5:30	241	7:40	173	9:50	134
1:20	994	3:30	379	5:40	234	7:50	169	10:00	133
1:30	884	3:40	361	5:50	227	8:00	166	10:10	130
1:40	797	3:50	346	6:00	221	8:10	162	10:20	128
1:50	723	4:00	331	6:10	215	8:20	159	10:30	126
2:00	663	4:10	318	6:20	209	8:30	156	10:40	124
2:10	612	4:20	306	6:30	204	8:40	153	10:50	122
2:20	568	4:30	295	6:40	199	8:50	150	11:00	120
2:30	530	4:40	284	6:50	194	9:00	147		
2:40	497	4:50	274	7:00	189	9:10	145		
2:50	468	5:00	265	7:10	185	9:20	142		
3:00	442	5:10	256	7:20	181	9:30	139		

A PRIMER FOR BABYSITTERS

How's your sitter safety rating?* On the job, do you know: How to keep children happily occupied and out of trouble? What to expect of babies and children at different ages? What to watch out for to prevent accidents? What to do and whom to call in any emergency? Even if you think you know all about baby-sitting, it will be worth your while to take a few moments to check up (and maybe brush up) on your practices.

If you have younger brothers and sisters at home, you probably feel confident and experienced. On the other hand, be frank about your qualifications. For instance, you won't want to accept a job caring for a young baby if you know nothing at all about infant care. It's best to gain your experience under a parent's supervision before taking full charge alone.

Safety Reminders for Different Ages

A good sitter watches the child *and* the surroundings. Although no two children are exactly alike, there is a predictable pattern of development which can help to guide your care.

Babies up to 6 Months

A newborn needs close attention and protection. Make sure that the baby's face is free of covers, clothing, or anything that might interfere with breathing. Take a look from time to time to make sure that he is resting comfortably, and also to see if more or fewer covers are needed. Even when adequately dressed and covered, a baby's hands usually stay cool. A better way to find out if he is warm enough is to feel arms, legs, or neck.

Remove your pins, bracelets, or any other jewelry which might bruise or scratch the baby. And put these fascinating trinkets where the infant cannot get them.

If you are expected to feed the baby, the parents should leave instructions. If you warm the bottle, test the milk—a drop or two on the inside of your wrist—to make sure that it is not hot. Babies can safely drink cool milk. (Better cold than hot!) Hold the baby cozily, in a semi-setting position, for feeding. Don't prop the bottle. If left alone, the baby might choke on the milk. To bring up air bubbles, burp the baby by holding him up against your shoulder. Do this before you put him back to bed so that he will be comfortable. When you pick up a young baby, be sure to support that wobbly head!

Babies should never be left on anything from which they might fall. Make it a habit to keep the sides of the crib up when not tending the baby. A brand-new baby can move considerably by kicking and wriggling. Even an infant who appears to be unable to move much may surprise you—the moment your back is turned—by tumbling off a bed, sofa, or table. So, never leave a baby unguarded even to get a fresh diaper or to answer the phone or doorbell.

Babies put things into their mouths. That's how they learn about taste, size, and the texture of things. Watch out for swallowable things—buttons, pins, beads, small detachable parts on toys. All potentially dangerous items—including your handbag and its contents—must be kept out of reach.

From 6 to 12 Months

At this age, babies begin to roll over, push backward and forward. They learn to sit, creep, crawl, and then pull up to a standing position. A crawling baby likes to get out of the playpen part of the time. It's the start of the "into everything" stage. When you let him out of the playpen, crib, or highchair, be alert to all possible danger in the way—breakable bric-a-brac, matches, and lighters on low tables and shelves, lamps and cords, electrical outlets, household cleansers, and medicines. If a baby grabs for a forbidden object, take it away matter-of-factly, and then divert attention to something else that's safe to have.

*Reprinted from *Health,* October 1976, by special permission. © 1976 Family Media, Inc. All rights reserved.

A baby may be shy or afraid when the parents first leave you together. Usually, you can help with gentle play or an interesting toy. But some parents prefer to have the sitter come to the house a few times to get acquainted with the baby in advance.

Babies in this age group usually enjoy games like pat-a-cake and peek-a-boo. They delight in dropping toys and watching you pick them up—a game that helps them to perfect their own muscle coordination. Toys that capture interest include small blocks, big bright wooden beads, rubber and plastic rings, large bells, and balls. Babies who seem bored with their current toy collection may welcome something different. Many household items make safe, intriguing playthings—pots and pans, soft plastic measuring cups and spoons, big wooden or plastic spools. Avoid sharp, breakable things or containers that have held dangerous substances, such as household cleansers.

From 12 to 15 Months

At this age, a child's curiosity seems boundless. Babies need to roam and explore, but they also need limits. You have to keep an eye on them practically all the time. Be sure that safety gates at top and bottom of stairways are latched. Without these, you may have to bar the stairs with a heavy chair, or what-have-you, to prevent climbing and falling.

Babies like to poke and probe. Getting into things is a natural part of learning, but it's up to *you* to watch for uncapped electric outlets, and the like, which baby might poke into. Make sure that low shelves do not contain harmful, breakable materials. Able to reach and pull, a baby can tug a tablecloth, and what's on it, *off* the table!

Toddlers, too, put things into their mouths. Scan surroundings for small, sharp objects. Make sure there are no poisonous substances—pesticides, household cleansers, bleaches, aspirin or medicines—within reach. Since toddlers climb, even cabinets above floor level may be within reach.

A baby of this age usually likes to play with simple toys that can be taken apart and put together again. With several blocks, the baby can put one on top of the other and knock them down.

Some babies and young children won't go to bed or take a nap without their favorite toy—usually a stuffed animal. You'll be wise to find out which toy is the special companion.

Around 2 Years

Two-year-olds are adventurous and independent. They know how to do many things and seldom sit still for a moment unless tired and sleepy. Turning a doorknob is a new skill that may mean trouble if, say, a cellar door is left unlocked. Or, in the blink of an eye, a child can be out the door and down the street! It happens all the time. So, besides being on the watch, make sure that doors leading to danger are locked.

This is also an age for much experimentation. A two-year-old enjoys taking things apart and putting them together again. Fine—so long as it isn't the TV set or Dad's electric razor! Safe, pull-apart, put-together toys are designed to intrigue children of this age, but everything else fascinates them, too. Don't let inquisitive fingers touch electrical equipment, mixers, and slicers. Watch out for matches and lighters. Since opening and closing drawers and cabinets is such great fun, you'll have to make certain that the contents are harmless.

Climbing is a favorite pastime, too. Do the windows have guards on them? If not, be sure they are locked or the screens fastened. Even at sleeptime, youngsters may clamber out to look around.

Two-year-olds can follow directions, but they resent and resist a steady stream of "don't," "no-no" and other commands. When there's plenty to do, the likelihood of getting into trouble is lessened. So, bring out their favorite toys to keep them interested and amused.

Around 3 Years

At this age, children have greater understanding and self-control and are usually cooperative.

A three-year-old is likely to be nimble and quick; he may hurry about, rushing up and down the stairs. Although they're fairly sure-footed, they should be reminded to always use the handrails.

Outdoors, hold the child's hand when near or crossing the street. Children of this age are so active and independent, they may dart away from you without thinking. Indoors, a child may like to look at picture books, play with peg boards, build with sturdy blocks. Sometimes, children just like to show you all their favorite toys or listen to you read a story.

Around 4 Years

A child of four may be very active—probably able to ride a tricycle or pedal car with ease. Remind the youngster to ride only on sidewalks and away from driveways.

He or she may like to play ball, throwing and catching. Caution the child to let the ball roll when it goes into the street and never to dart after it without looking.

Four-year-olds are great climbers. It's best if they can indulge in this sport in a suitable place—preferably a play area equipped with climbing apparatus. Still, they need to be watched, especially when playing where larger, older children are sharing the swings, seesaws, and jungle gyms. Bigger children sometimes get too rough for the little ones.

For quiet play, you can interest a four-year-old with books, finger paints, clay, crayons and coloring books, chalk and chalkboards, blunt scissors, paper and paste.

From 5 to 7 Years

These children are not babies (and won't like to be treated as such), but they still need a sitter when their parents are away. You have to be on hand to help—to offer reminders and suggestions—then step aside when the child seems to be doing all right.

Children of these ages usually can do a pretty good job of dressing themselves without much assistance. And they are generally cooperative about picking up and putting away their toys and games.

Essay Questions: On a sheet of paper answer the following questions:

1. What kind of behavior does the author tell you to expect from a two-year-old?
2. Why did the author write this article?
3. If you were preparing to babysit a child of four years of age, what kind of activities would you plan?

Check your answers with those found in Appendix B.

Vocabulary Exercise: On a sheet of paper, place the letter of the best answer next to the number for each vocabulary word.

1. surroundings
   "A good sitter watches the child and the surroundings. . . ."
   a. parents in the home
   b. area around the child
   c. pets and furnishings
   d. neighborhood

2. adequately

"Even when adequately dressed and covered. . . ."

   a. sufficiently
   b. warmly
   c. lightly
   d. heavily

3. nimble

"A three year old is likely to be nimble and quiet. . . ."

   a. surefooted
   b. awkward
   c. careful
   d. cooperative

4. clamber

"Even at sleeptime, youngsters may clamber out to look. . . ."

   a. run
   b. struggle
   c. hurry
   d. climb

5. potentially

"All potentially dangerous items should be moved. . . ."

   a. can develop into
   b. usually seen as
   c. unknown as
   d. rarely happens

6. intriguing

"Many household items make safe, intriguing playthings. . . ."

   a. harmless
   b. soft
   c. interesting
   d. dangerous

7. detachable

"Small detachable parts of toys can be. . . ."

   a. unbreakable
   b. removable
   c. sharp
   d. fastened

Check your answers with those in Appendix B.

Time Conversion Chart

Min:Sec	WPM	Min:Sec	WPM	Min:Sec	WPM	Min:Sec	WPM	Min:Sec	WPM
1:00	1930	4:40	414	8:20	232	12:00	161	15:40	123
1:10	1654	4:50	399	8:30	227	12:10	159	15:50	122
1:20	1448	5:00	386	8:40	223	12:20	156	16:00	121
1:30	1287	5:10	374	8:50	218	12:30	154	16:10	119
1:40	1158	5:20	362	9:00	214	12:40	152	16:20	118
1:50	1053	5:30	351	9:10	211	12:50	150	16:30	117
2:00	965	5:40	341	9:20	207	13:00	148	16:40	116
2:10	891	5:50	331	9:30	203	13:10	147	16:50	115
2:20	827	6:00	322	9:40	200	13:20	145	17:00	114
2:30	772	6:10	313	9:50	196	13:30	143	17:10	112
2:40	724	6:20	305	10:00	193	13:40	141	17:20	111
2:50	681	6:30	297	10:10	190	13:50	140	17:30	110
3:00	643	6:40	290	10:20	187	14:00	138	17:40	109
3:10	609	6:50	282	10:30	184	14:10	136	17:50	108
3:20	579	7:00	276	10:40	181	14:20	135	18:00	107
3:30	551	7:10	269	10:50	178	14:30	133	18:10	106
3:40	526	7:20	263	11:00	175	14:40	132	18:20	105
3:50	503	7:30	257	11:10	173	14:50	130	18:30	104
4:00	483	7:40	252	11:20	170	15:00	129	18:40	103
4:10	463	7:50	246	11:30	168	15:10	127	18:50	102
4:20	445	8:00	241	11:40	165	15:20	126	19:00	102
4:30	429	8:10	236	11:50	163	15:30	125	19:10	101
								19:20	100

Reading Rate Improvement

How Can You Improve Your Reading Rate?

Many programs advocate the ability to increase your reading rate by three or four times the rate you are reading at the present time. Unfortunately this probably will not happen. Research indicates a limit as to the number of words your eyes can see. Consequently, don't expect to be able to read whole lines or even large phrases at a glance. Rather, expect to increase your reading rate at a reasonable level.

While reading, your eyes have to pause to see the words. This pause is called a *fixation*. The more fixations per second the faster you read. Some students experience about four fixations per second. Very good readers can do a little better with about five fixations per second. Thus, to expect large gains in reading rate is not realistic. What is realistic is to know that you can adjust your reading rate from subject to subject. By doing this you become a flexible reader; that is, one who can decide how to go about the reading task at hand. If you are able to do this successfully, you will see your reading rate and comprehension improve.

The key to improving your reading rate is practice. You need to experience increasing your fixation rate. To do this, you need to practice reading your textbook material in a timed setting. Your teacher will assist you with this.

What Do You Need to Do to Increase Your Reading Rate?

Rate-boost exercises are not the same as regular reading. In regular reading you adjust your reading rate to achieve comprehension of the material. When doing rate-boost exercises, you let comprehension drop while increasing rate. Letting go of comprehension is absolutely necessary with rate-boost exercises. Doing so means going against what you have been told about reading for understanding. But if you try this procedure, you will see your comprehension begin to rise as your mind adapts to higher speeds.

What Will Happen to Your Comprehension When You Do Rate-Boost Exercises?

At first you will want to read at slower rates in order to have good understanding. But you must let that go! Read at rates that cause you to answer about one-half of the questions correctly. By practicing at higher reading rates for a time, you will begin to adjust your reading rate for the different subjects you are studying.

How Can You Chart Your Progress?

A rate-boost progress chart is provided for you. After each timed reading, chart your reading rate (WPM) and the number of correct responses. Remember, you should allow your comprehension to drop when practicing rate improvement exercises. To time your reading, put down your starting time. When you complete the reading put down your ending time. Later go back and see what your reading time is. Look at the Time Conversion Chart provided for the reading. Record your time and score on the Reading Rate Improvement Chart found in the *Student Activity Booklet* on page 81.

DISEASE

The word "disease" literally means to feel "not at ease."* If a person has some type of disease, he will, in fact, not feel well. Today the word "disease" has been broadened to mean that one or more organs in the body are not functioning as they should. The disease may be caused by any number of things. It can also be classified in different ways.

Disease that is present at birth may be classified as either hereditary or congenital. A disease which is passed through the genes from parent to child is an inherited disease. Allergies and color-blindness are examples of such a disease. However, they do not always show up in every child or in every generation. A congenital disease is caused when a baby does not form normally while inside the mother's body. It may be born with heart valves that do not work well or with other disorders such as clubfoot or harelip. These defects can usually be corrected through surgery.

Infectious diseases include those caused when germs enter the body. A germ is a tiny plant or animal that can only be seen by a microscope. When certain kinds of germs grow inside the body, they can damage body tissue and cause a person to become ill. Many infectious diseases can be passed from a sick person to a healthy one. These types are called contagious or communicable diseases. Measles, mumps, and influenza are examples of such diseases.

The body itself works to prevent disease from occurring. It has a system of natural defenses. One of the most important of these is the skin. The skin serves as a barrier to many agents that cause illness when they enter the body. This is why a cut or break in the skin can make a person more susceptible, or likely, to catch some disease. Other natural defenses include fluids which are produced by the body. An example is stomach acid which kills many types of bacteria that enter the body through food that is eaten. The sense of pain, coughing, and sneezing are natural body reactions that also protect the body from harm.

If the body does become ill with a disease, it will naturally begin to fight it by making more white blood cells. These cells fight the infection and help the body to become well again. When the body is unable to produce enough natural protection, a doctor can prescribe various types of drugs that will help the body combat most diseases.

A doctor can also provide certain types of medicine that will prevent disease from occurring. One way of doing this is through vaccination, or inoculation, for particular diseases. A vaccine is usually made from dead or weakened germs that cause a certain disease. When these are placed in a healthy person's body, the body will make substances called antibodies that fight the disease. These antibodies stay in the blood and protect the person from the disease. People who have received certain types of vaccinations are usually immune from those particular diseases, meaning that they will not reoccur. If the disease does reoccur, it will probably not be as severe. Several dreaded diseases which caused many deaths in the past are now under control largely through development of vaccines.

Comprehension Questions: On a separate sheet of paper, write the correct answer to each question.

1. The term "disease" basically means that:

    a. a person feels rotten and needs to see a doctor
    b. it can be spread from one person to another person
    c. one or more organs in the body are not functioning as they should
    d. people are born with defects that result in pain

2. A person's body will fight a disease by:

    a. producing complex chemicals to combat the illness
    b. producing more white blood cells
    c. introducing red blood cells to the affected area
    d. producing antibodies

3. Several body reactions that protect the body from harm are:

    a. nervousness and arm movement
    b. pain and drowsiness
    c. muscle spasms and vomiting
    d. coughing and sneezing

4. What is one way a medical doctor can prevent disease?

Answer Key:

1) c   2) b   3) d   4) Answers will vary.

Time Conversion Chart

Min:Sec	WPM	Min:Sec	WPM	Min:Sec	WPM	Min:Sec	WPM	Min:Sec	WPM
0:30	1100	1:20	413	2:10	254	3:00	183	3:50	143
0:40	825	1:30	367	2:20	236	3:10	174	4:00	137
0:50	660	1:40	330	2:30	220	3:20	165		
1:00	550	1:50	300	2:40	206	3:30	157		
1:10	471	2:00	275	2:50	194	3:40	150		

TSUNAMIS: OCEAN WAVES OF DEATH AND DESTRUCTION
by Ronald Fenton

Every island and coastal settlement in the Pacific Ocean area is vulnerable to the on-slaught of seismic sea-waves, the destructive oceanic offspring of earthquakes (or seisms) and volcanic eruption.*

Some call them "tidal waves," a name as misleading as it has been persistent: these great waves are not caused by tides. The Japanese, whose islands have felt the destructive power of the great waves for generations, give us the name used internationally: tsunami.

In 1868 and 1877 tsunamis devastated towns in northern Chile, and caused death and damage across the Pacific. A series of seismic sea-waves generated by the eruption and collapse of Krakatoa in 1883 killed more than 36,000 persons in the East Indies. Japan lost 27,000 lives to the wave of 1896, and 1,000 more to that of 1933. There have been hundreds more whose effects were less spectacular but which took many lives and did much damage.

Tsunamis occur most often in the Pacific. Around this immense ocean runs a zone of extreme seismic activity crowned by a volcanic "Ring of Fire."

This seismic belt extends along the major geologic faults, or fractures, and the deep oceanic trenches of South and Central America and the United States, turning westward along the Aleutian Island arc, then southward through Japan and the Philippine Republic; here it branches westward to Malaysia and Indonesia, and eastward through New Guinea, the south-ern island groups, and New Zealand.

The phenomenon we call "tsunami" is a series of travelling ocean waves of extremely long length and period. In the deep ocean, their length from crest to crest may be a hundred miles or more, their height from trough to crest only a few feet.

They cannot be felt aboard ships in deep water, and they cannot be seen from the air. But the kinetic energy—the energy of movement—represented by a tsunami is impressive: a tsunami "feels the bottom" even in the deepest ocean, and it appears that the progress of this imperceptible series of waves represents the movement of the entire verticle section of ocean through which the tsunami passes. In the deep ocean they may even reach speeds of over 900 km. per hour.

As the tsunami enters the shoaling water of coastlines in its path, the velocity of its waves diminishes and wave height increases. It is in these shallow waters that tsunamis become a threat of life and property, for they can crest to heights of more than 30 metres and strike with devastating force.

Tsunamis are believed to originate as displaced columns of ocean water, but the displac-ing agent has not been positively identified. Seismic or volcanic alterations of the ocean floor, provided they impart some vertical movement to the water column, may cause tsunamis. Sub-marine avalanches on the slopes of the Pacific trenches may also produce tsunamis.

Although it has been established that a relationship exists between seismic or volcanic disturbances and tsunamis, the nature of this relationship is not well-defined. Tsunami mag-nitude appears to be a function of earthquake magnitude and depth, water depth where the tsunami is generated and the extent to which the earth's crust is deformed by the earthquake. But the combined effect of these factors is still imperfectly understood.

The speed of tsunamis varies with water depth, and it is this relationship which permits prediction of tsunami arrival times at all points in the Pacific Ocean area.

A tsunami warning system and an international tsunami information centre serving all areas of the Pacific have been set up at Honolulu, capital of Hawaii. Their work has done much to reduce the hazards of the tsunami—the most destructive of all waves.

*Reprinted from the *Unesco Chronicle*, May 1976.

Using seismographs and tide-gauges scientists are able to predict almost exactly when a tsunami will arrive at a given seacoast since tsunamis are known to travel at speeds that may average from 650 to 800 kilometres an hour, the exact speed depending on the depth of water over which they pass.

But it is still not possible to predict what effect the topography of the ocean floor will have on a tsunami. It is not completely clear, for example, why a tsunami's wave may be of negligible size at one beach, and of giant proportions a few miles away.

What is certain, however, is that all tsunamis—like hurricanes—are potentially dangerous, even though they may not strike each Pacific coastline or do damage at each coastline they strike. So a constant tsunami watch has to be kept and the peoples of the Pacific alerted when the great waves roll across the world's largest ocean.

Comprehension Questions: Circle the letter of the best answer.

1. The word tsunami came from the:

  a. Dutch
  b. Japanese
  c. Hawaiians
  d. Polynesians

2. Tsunamis can be:

  a. seen from the air
  b. felt by ships in deep water
  c. detected by ocean watchers
  d. destructive to oceanside dwellers

3. The most common name for tsunamis is:

  a. hurricane
  b. typhoon
  c. earthquake
  d. tidal wave

4. How can tsunamis be predicted?

Answer Key:
1) b   2) d   3) d   4) By using a seismograph scientists can predict when a tsunami will arrive.

Time Conversion Chart

Min:Sec	WPM	Min:Sec	WPM	Min:Sec	WPM	Min:Sec	WPM	Min:Sec	WPM
1:00	770	1:40	462	2:20	330	3:00	257	3:40	210
1:10	660	1:50	420	2:30	308	3:10	243	3:50	201
1:20	578	2:00	385	2:40	289	3:20	231	4:00	193
1:30	513	2:10	355	2:50	272	3:30	220		

MONEY

Before money was common, people used a system of barter to get the things they needed and wanted.* "Barter" means "to trade" and early societies used this method of exchange for many years. For example, if a man had some chickens, perhaps he could trade these for some flour. This system of exchanging what was not needed, or surplus, for what was needed, was simple. The problem with such a system, however, was that the man had to find someone who had what he wanted and who, in turn, wanted what he had. A second problem was in deciding how much flour was equal in value to how many chickens. Thus the barter system was many times a very awkward way of conducting business.

People soon discovered that some things held more value because they were things everyone wanted or needed. Thus, these common articles became a medium of exchange, or money. At different times and places such things as shells, beads, furs, whale teeth, tobacco, guns, copper, iron, silver, and gold have been accepted in payment for goods and services and in payment of debts.

Eventually metals came to be used as a medium of exchange. At first this metal was in the form of dust, lumps, or bars. It was necessary to weigh or measure it each time it was used. The answer to this problem was to make the metal into some standard shape, weight, and size. Thus, coins came into existence.

We are not certain when the first metal coins were used. The Bible mentions "pieces of silver." There have been some coins found that were believed to have been made about 700 B.C. in Asia Minor. The drachma was a silver coin used by the Greeks, and the Romans used silver coins, also, during the time of the Roman Empire.

The use of coins had many advantages. It could be carrried more easily than some articles of exchange—livestock for example. Each piece could be given a set value. Uneven exchanges could be made and trade could be better standardized.

Paper money did not become commonly used until around the 17th century. However, some historians believe it was used in China as early as the 10th century. Usually this paper was a written promise to pay someone. If the person making the promise was honest, the system worked well. People also found paper even more convenient than coins to carry and store.

The United States government did not begin making paper currency until 1861. The coin and paper money issued by our government is a "token" money. That is, the coins contain less actual value in metal than the value stamped on it. Also, the government does not promise any longer to pay the amounts of the paper bill in silver or gold. The reason this system can work is because of the stability of the economy and the faith of people in the system.

Today another kind of monitary system exists that has become so widespread that it will probably make currency obsolete in the near future. This is the check and credit card system. The majority of business transactions in our world today use this system. Convenience is again a major reason. Economists predict that soon everyone will have a credit card and all transactions will be done by computers.

Comprehension Questions: Circle the letter of the best answer.

1. In the days before money was used, people:
    a. used gold to pay for goods and services
    b. used paper bills to pay for goods and services
    c. worked for one another to pay off debtors
    d. traded things to get what they needed and wanted

2. The coin and paper money used in the United States is called token money because:
    a. the coins and paper money are worth more than their face value
    b. the coins and paper money are worth less than their face value
    c. the gold and silver backing the money is worth more
    d. credit cards and checking accounts have replaced street currency

3. The reason for the use of credit cards is:
    a. it is cheaper
    b. it is more convenient
    c. it is faster
    d. it causes less paper work

4. Where did paper money become used regularly as a way to pay for goods and services?

Answer Key:
1) d   2) b   3) b   4) Paper money became commonly used around the 17th century.

Time Conversion Chart

Min:Sec	WPM	Min:Sec	WPM	Min:Sec	WPM	Min:Sec	WPM	Min:Sec	WPM
0:30	1126	1:20	422	2:10	260	3:00	188	3:50	147
0:40	845	1:30	375	2:20	241	3:10	178	4:00	141
0:50	676	1:40	338	2:30	225	3:20	169		
1:00	563	1:50	307	2:40	211	3:30	161		
1:10	483	2:00	282	2:50	199	3:40	154		

STRETCH YOUR IMAGINATION

Most of the writing you do in school is **realistic;** that is, you write about things that have actually happened or are likely to happen.* These things are "real"—or could be. A story may thus be realistic even though it is make-believe. There is, however, writing which is not meant to portray things as they are in real life. You may have read something like the following excerpt, something you know could not actually happen:

> "Have some mustard," said the magician, . . .
> The mustard-pot got up and walked over to his plate on thin silver legs that waddled like the owl's. Then it uncurled its handles and one handle lifted its lid with exaggerated courtesy while the other helped him to a generous spoonful.
> "Oh, I love the mustard-pot!" cried the Wart. "Wherever did you get it?"
> At this the pot beamed all over its face and began to strut a bit, but Merlyn rapped it on the head with a teaspoon, so that it sat down and shut up at once.
> "It is not a bad pot," he said grudgingly. "Only it is inclined to give itself airs."
> —T. H. White,
>   *The Once and Future King*

In this excerpt, a magician named Merlyn and a boy named Wart are eating lunch together, a realistic situation. But then what happens? What elements show that the author stretched his imagination beyond reality? Unrealistic writing like this is often called **fantasy.** It goes beyond what could possibly happen in real life to what could only happen in one's imagination.

Fantasy has always been popular among writers. There are, however, no set rules for writing fantasy. In fact, the only limitations placed upon writing fantasy are those placed by the writer's own imagination. Perhaps no other writing demands so much. It is easy to fantasize—many of our daydreams are pure fantasy. It is harder to shape and express those fantasies in words, but it can be challenging and rewarding to do so. Much of the world's great literature uses fantasy. For example, a famous story like "Rip Van Winkle":

> He looked round for his gun, but in place of the clean, well-oiled fowling-piece, he found an old firelock lying by him, the barrel incrusted with rust, the lock falling off, and the stock worm-eaten. . . .
> . . . [T]o his astonishment, he found his beard had grown a foot long!
> —Washington Irving,
>   "Rip Van Winkle"

Fantasy may appear in a novel as it does in *Gulliver's Travels:*

> In a little time I felt something alive moving on my left leg; . . . when bending my eyes downward as much as I could, I perceived it to be a human creature not six inches high, with a bow and arrow in his hands and a quiver on his back.
> —Jonathan Swift,
>   *Gulliver's Travels*

*By permission of LAIDLAW BROTHERS, A Division of Doubleday & Company, Inc.

A writer may use fantasy in the form of a poem or a limerick as Edward Lear did.

> There was a Young Lady of Norway,
> Who casually sat in a doorway;
> When the door squeezed her flat,
>   she exclaimed, "What of that?"
> This courageous Young Lady of Norway.
>   —Edward Lear

Many television shows are built on fantasy. *I Dream of Jeannie* and *Bewitched* are recent examples. If you watch television, especially on Saturday mornings, you can probably think of others.

What do these different uses of fantasy have in common? Any kind of writing demands a use of imagination, of course, but fantasy demands that the writer stretch his imagination beyond actual human experience. You probably noticed also that each of the examples combines fantasy with reality. Fantasy is most effective—and most enjoyable—when it shows a contrast between what is likely and what is unlikely, between what man can know and what he can only dream.

Comprehension Questions: Circle the letter of the best answer.

1. The main theme discussed in this passage was:
   a. stories about fantacies
   b. stories about real people
   c. applying stories to your life
   d. using your imagination

2. An application of "fantasy" as described in the passage was:
   a. radio programs
   b. story telling
   c. group discussions
   d. TV programs

3. In writing fantasy the writers:
   a. follow specific rules about how to write these types of stories
   b. are free to do what they want in writing
   c. use as much realism as possible in the stories
   d. create fictional characters to liven up the stories

4. Where is the use of fantasy most effective?

Answer Key:
1) d   2) d   3) b   4) When a contrast between what is likely and what is unlikely is used.

Time Conversion Chart

Min:Sec	WPM	Min:Sec	WPM	Min:Sec	WPM	Min:Sec	WPM	Min:Sec	WPM
0:30	1230	1:20	461	2:10	284	3:00	205	3:50	160
0:40	923	1:30	410	2:20	264	3:10	194	4:00	154
0:50	738	1:40	369	2:30	246	3:20	185		
1:00	615	1:50	335	2:40	231	3:30	176		
1:10	527	2:00	308	2:50	217	3:40	168		

HOW CAN YOU BECOME PHYSICALLY FIT?

Physical fitness is for everybody, not just for athletes.* If you are physically fit, you are in the best possible condition for you. You have energy for the things you want to do. You can take part in games and sports without getting too tired. You eat better, sleep better, and look better when you are physically fit.

Regular exercise each day will help you become physically fit. Regular exercise helps you stay in top condition. It helps your heart and lungs become stronger and more efficient. It will help your muscles develop firmness or tone.

Team sports such as football, basketball, and baseball appeal to many young people. But there are many activities that need only one or two people. Which ones appeal to you?

When you exercise each day, you are forming a very good habit. It is a habit that will be important to you all your life. It can help you avoid *atherosclerosis*. This is a condition that leads to heart disease. In atherosclerosis, fatty deposits clog the arteries of the heart. As a result, the heart must pump harder to supply the body with blood.

Regular exercise can help you avoid becoming *obese,* or extremely fat. Obesity is a serious problem for about three million American teen-agers. A research study of young people who were obese revealed surprising facts. The young people studied were found to eat *less* than young people of normal weight. In fact, they ate about 350 calories a day less! But they exercised very little. They were three times less active than teen-agers of normal weight.

In another study, a group of teen-agers *doubled* the amount of food they ate daily. Yet they did not gain weight. They accomplished this by increasing their physical activity.

Of course, when you exercise strenuously, you may eat somewhat more. This is necessary to maintain your body's weight. During periods of growth, the body needs extra energy. Still, a person who daily eats more than his or her body needs can expect the extra colories to go into fat. The key to effective weight control is to find a balance between how much you eat and how much you exercise. This is true at all ages.

How much exercise you need is an individual matter. It is a good idea to push yourself a little each day. Exercise to the point of getting tired, but not exhausted. This is called the *overload principle.* Each day you overload the body with a little extra exercise. Gradually you become able to function well during the school day and still have extra energy for work and play after school.

It is also a good idea to develop skill in a favorite sport or game. When you do this, you are likely to enjoy exercise more and to keep at it.

If you want to include more than one kind of activity, you might do some exercises. This way you can strengthen different muscles of your body.

*From "How Can You Become Physically Fit?" by Julius B. Richmond. American Medical Association, Chicago, Ill. Reprinted by permission.

Comprehension Questions: On a separate sheet of paper, write the correct answer to each question.

1. Physical fitness is:

    a. for athletes only
    b. for sports minded people
    c. something to be avoided
    d. for everyone of all ages

2. Regular exercise is good because it:

    a. keeps your mind occupied for awhile each day
    b. helps your muscles stay in shape
    c. gives you a great deal of pleasure
    d. creates special chemicals in your body

3. If you eat more than you need you can expect:

    a. to burn it off easily
    b. the extra calories to go into fat
    c. the new calories to go into muscle
    d. that regular exercise will keep you slim

4. How long should you exercise before stopping?

Answer Key:
1) d   2) b   3) b   4) You should continue until you have completed your routine.

Time Conversion Chart

Min:Sec	WPM	Min:Sec	WPM	Min:Sec	WPM	Min:Sec	WPM	Min:Sec	WPM
0:30	1500	1:20	563	2:10	346	3:00	250	3:50	196
0:40	1125	1:30	500	2:20	321	3:10	237	4:00	188
0:50	900	1:40	450	2:30	300	3:20	225		
1:00	750	1:50	410	2:40	281	3:30	214		
1:10	643	2:00	375	2:50	265	3:40	205		

Appendix A
Are You a Victim of Word Overload?

As a student you are constantly being introduced to new words. You go to your mathematics class and hear such terms as *obtuse, acute,* and *supplementary.* Then you go on to science where you might see *dispersion, combustion,* and *kinetic.* In geography class you read about *apex, piedmont, topography.* In English class, the story you are reading describes people as being *amiable, neurotic, incredulous.* New words will also be introduced in History, P.E., Health, Home Economics, Industrial Arts, Music or any other class you are taking.

With so many new words to learn, it is easy for you to become "overloaded." You won't always have time to run to the dictionary to find the definition for a new word and there won't always be a glossary in the back of your book. So what will you do? Overlook it? We hope not! Chances are you will see the word again. If you do not do something to make that word or words a part of your vocabulary now, it might mean you will lose some important information later.

In this section, you will learn about various ways to add to your present vocabulary. One of our goals is for you to discover that the study of words is fun and interesting. It is more than turning to a dictionary whenever you come across an unfamiliar word. There is an extra bonus waiting for those who follow through with the program—your reading and learning will be a much more pleasurable and rewarding experience.

ASK yourself these questions:

Do I use a vocabulary file in learning new words?
Do I look for context clues to help me learn the meaning of new words?
Do I know how to use the dictionary?
Do I know how to use a Thesaurus?
DO I know how to use the Synonym Finder?

How Can You Build Your Word Power?

Your most valuable tool in building "WORD POWER" will be your vocabulary file. We suggest you begin by buying some 3″ × 5″ index cards. The 3 × 5 cards are easy to handle. They can be kept together with rubber bands and can be carried in your pocket. To make a more organized system, colored cards are helpful. By using colored cards, you can color code your words and put math words on blue, science on yellow, English on white cards, etc.

Your next step will be to record your new words on the cards as you come upon them in your listening and reading. On the top of your card, write the word. Below it write the sentence or part of the sentence which contains the word. You may want to also write down what you think the word means. Then, go to your dictionary and look up the word. Write the definition on the card. If several definitions are given, write the one that applies to your sentence. Include information such as what part of speech the word is, any spelling changes that are made when a prefix or suffix is added or examples that will help you better understand the definition. Here is an example:

```
FORM
   The men had to build a form
before laying the concrete for the
sidewalk.




Noun = a mold (15 other definitions)
```

How Can Context Clues Help You?

Authors are not out to make learning difficult by giving you new words. If you look carefully at sentences containing new words, you often find clues the author has given you in that sentence to help you understand their meanings. Even if you can't find help in the sentence itself, there will likely be information around the sentence which will give you some idea of what the word means.

EXERCISE A.1   Look at each of the sentences below. The word in *italics* may or may not be familiar to you. Read the sentence and write a possible definition for each *italicized* word. Answer on separate sheet of paper.

Example: The **meandering** stream wound its way through the forest.

Definition: *Meandering means winding*

(1) Please **note** on your paper the differences between the Civil War and the Mexican-American War.

Definition: _____

(2) Food coloring will **diffuse** and spread throughout the mixture.

Definition: _____

(3) A **goiter** is a swelling of the glands in the front part and side of the neck.

Definition: _____

(4) If the experiment doesn't work the first time, you may want to **replicate** it.

Definition: _____

(5) Please present your word in a **legible**, easy-to-read format.

Definition: _____

(6) **A perennial** plant does not die at the end of its growing season.

Definition: _____

Check your answers with those found in Appendix B.

The clues that help you figure out the meanings of new words are called *CONTEXT CLUES*. *Context* is the part of a passage that helps to explain the new word it includes.

Many times context clues are in the form of *synonyms*. Synonyms are words that have the same or close to the same meaning as another word. In the exercise above, many of your clues came from synonyms. For instance, look again at the example in EXERCISE A.1. The synonym for *meandering* is *wound* or *winding*. In the remaining sentences, can you identify two synonym pairs from among them?
Were your pairs any of the following?

diffuse–spread
goiter–swelling
legible–easy-to-read

How Can You Use the Dictionary, Thesaurus, and Synonym Finders?

Many times you will come across words in your reading that you won't be able to identify using context clues or other synonyms. One strategy you have been taught to use is a dictionary. Most of you are probably familiar with using an *abridged* version of a dictionary. An abridged dictionary includes only the more common words in our language. The entries for each word are brief and usually include a pronunciation guide, parts of speech, definitions, and examples of ways the word can be used. The following is an entry from *WEBSTER'S NEW WORLD DICTIONARY OF THE AMERICAN LANGUAGE:*

> **form** (form) *n.* [<L. *forma*] 1. Shape; general structure 2. the figure of a person or animal 3. a mold 4. a particular mode, kind, type, etc. [ice is a *form* of water; the *forms* of poetry] 5. arrangement; style 6. a way of doing something requiring skill 7. a customary or conventional procedure; formality; ceremony 8. a printed document with blanks to be filled in 9. condition of mind or body 10. a chart giving information about horses in a race 11. a changed appearance of a word to show inflection, etc. 12. type, etc. locked in a frame for pickling—*vt.* 1. to shape; fashion 2. to train; instruct 3. to develop (habits) 4. to make up; constitute—*vi.* to be formed.

As you see, the word *form* has many definitions and uses. This dictionary also tells us a short *etymology* or indication of the word's origin. How well do you understand the above entry?

EXERCISE A.2 On a sheet of paper answer the following questions?
(1) From what language did *form* evolve, Latin or Greek?

_____

(2) How many parts of speech are listed for *form*?

_____ What are they? _____

(3) Which definition includes an example?

_____

Check your answers with those found in Appendix B.

121

¹form \ˈfȯ(ə)rm, -ȯ(ə)m\ *n* -s *often attrib* [ME *forme, fourme,* fr. OF, fr. L *forma,* perh. modif. of Gk *morphē;* perh. akin to Gk *marmairein* to flash, sparkle — more at MORN] **1** *obs* **:** IMAGE, REPRESENTATION **2 a :** the shape and structure of something as distinguished from the material of which it is composed ⟨the carefully graded ~ of the curves⟩ **b :** a body esp. of a human being as distinguished (1) by external appearance or (2) from the countenance or visage **:** FIGURE ⟨the dress displayed her ~ to advantage⟩ **c** *archaic* **:** pleasing external appearance **:** BEAUTY ⟨he had no ~ or comeliness —Isa 53:2 (RSV)⟩ **3 a :** the ideal or intrinsic character of anything or something that imposes this character; *sometimes* **:** a pattern or schema **b** *in metaphysics* **:** the essential nature of a thing as distinguished from the matter in which this is embodied: as (1) *in Platonic philosophy* **:** a transcendent idea, universal essence, or subsistent entity (2) *in Aristotelian or scholastic philosophy* **:** the component of a thing that determines it in its kind or species **:** FORMAL CAUSE — often distinguished from *matter* (3) *in Baconian philosophy* **:** the basis constituting the condition for the existence of any given nature or quality (as density, heat, or color) **c** *in Kantian philosophy* **:** one of the formative modes of perception and cognition regarded as a subjective factor molding reality as given in sensation into systematic experience esp. as regards spatial and temporal order **4 a** *obs* **:** manner, method, or style (as of proceeding) **b :** established method of expression or practice **:** fixed or formal way of proceeding **:** procedure according to rule or rote **c :** a prescribed and usu. set order of words **:** FORMULA ⟨the ~ of the marriage service in the prayer book⟩ **d** *obs* **:** RECIPE, PRESCRIPTION **e** (1) **:** a printed or typed document with blank spaces for insertion of required or requested specific information ⟨a ~ for a deed⟩ ⟨be sure to fill all blanks on your tax ~⟩ (2) **:** a document of this kind which is attached to and forms an endorsement of a property insurance policy and in which is filled in a description of the property insured; *broadly* **:** such an endorsement containing alterations or modifications of the provisions of a standard policy **5 a :** conduct regulated by extraneous controls (as of custom or etiquette) **:** CEREMONY, CONVENTIONALITY, FORMALITY; *sometimes* **:** show without substance **:** empty pretentious appearance or ceremony **b :** a prescribed manner of behaving (as in society) ⟨the rigid ~ of the imperial court⟩ **:** an act of conduct or mode of procedure prescribed (as by custom or a code of etiquette) ⟨the complex ~*s* and taboos of the savage⟩ **:** FORMALITY, CEREMONY, CONVENTIONALITY ⟨knew all the ~*s* for wooing a proper young miss⟩ **c :** manner or conduct as tested by a prescribed or accepted standard — used with a qualifying adjective ⟨his behavior was often bad ~⟩ ⟨such poor ~ is to be deplored⟩ **d :** manner or style of performing or accomplishing something esp. when recognized standards of technique exist ⟨he is a strong swimmer but weak on ~⟩ **6 a :** the resting place of a hare or occas. of another animal **b :** a long seat **:** JOINT STOOL, BENCH ⟨seated on a low ~ against the wall⟩ **c :** a supporting frame model of the human figure or other device used for displaying merchandise in a store; *also* **:** a proportioned and often adjustable model for fitting clothes **d :** something that holds, supports, and gives or determines shape; *esp* **:** a mold in which concrete is placed to set **7** *obs* **a :** degree of quality, dignity, eminence, or excellence **b :** a class or rank esp. in society or official life **8 a :** the total combination of the letterpress matter imposed and locked up in a chase with the furniture, quoins, and the chase itself **b :** set-up type ⟨how to move ~*s* from the galley to the stone⟩ ⟨wind the cord clockwise around the ~⟩ **9 a :** one of the different modes of existence, action, or manifestation of a particular thing or substance **:** KIND, MODIFICATION, SPECIES, VARIETY ⟨the diamond, graphite, and soot are allotropic ~*s* of carbon⟩ ⟨the democratic ~ of government⟩ ⟨one ~ of respiratory disorder⟩ ⟨the ~ of vegetation typical of xerophytic areas⟩ **b** *also* **for·ma** \-mə\ **:** a botanical taxonomic category ranking below a variety and consisting of individuals that differ from those of related forms in one or very few characters ⟨the *discretiflorus* ~ of the rush *Juncus tenuis*⟩; *also* **:** a member of such a category **c :** a distinguishable group of organisms — commonly used by zoologists to avoid taxonomic implications ⟨the southern ~ of the hairy woodpecker⟩ **10 a :** orderly arrangement or method of arrangement (as in the presentation of ideas) **:** manner of coordinating elements (as of an artistic production or course of reasoning); *sometimes* **:** a particular kind or instance of such arrangement ⟨the sonnet is a poetical ~⟩ **b** *in logic* (1) **:** the structure, pattern, or schema possessed in common by different logical statements esp. as disclosed through the substitution of variables for different descriptive terms so that the manner in which the terms are interrelated becomes apparent (2) **:** the structure of an argument or an inference as symbolized by the use of variables (3) **:** the logical properties of a word, expression, or symbol as exhibited by its contribution to the logical form of statements in which it may properly occur **c :** the structural element, plan, or design of a work of art; *specif* **:** the combinations and relations to each other of various components (as lines, colors, and volumes in a visual work of art or themes and elaborations in an aural work of art) ⟨~ consists in a pattern of relationships that gives unity to a complex of perceptual elements —F.S.Haserot⟩ — often contrasted with *content* **d :** a relationship between or among elements of raw subject matter (as in a painting) which is sensed and made structural by the artist; *also* **:** a visible and measurable unit defined by a contour **:** a bounded surface or volume or a system of visible elements **e** (1) **:** the structural pattern of a musical composition (2) **:** a specific type (as fugue, rondo, sonata) of such pattern **11 :** a class or grade in a British secondary school or in certain American private schools — see SIXTH FORM **12 a :** the past performance of a race horse; *often* **:** a table giving details relating to a horse's past performance (as handicaps, jockeys, odds) used by bettors in making selections ⟨a ~ sheet⟩ ⟨a racing ~⟩ ⟨~ players⟩ **b :** CONDITION, FITNESS ⟨preseason workouts to get in ~ for the regular season⟩; *often* **:** known ability to perform ⟨a batter off his ~ at the plate⟩ ⟨a musician playing at the top of his ~⟩ **13 :** the combination of faces included under a general crystallographic symbol and necessary to satisfy the symmetry of the crystal ⟨a single crystal often exhibits faces of two or more crystal ~*s* which supplement one another or truncate one another's edges or corners⟩ **14 a :** LINGUISTIC FORM **b :** one of the different aspects a word may take as a result of inflection or change of spelling or pronunciation ⟨obsolete, participial, or verbal ~*s*⟩ **15** *math* **:** a rational integral homogeneous function of a set of variables **16 :** the immature flower bud of the cotton plant **17 :** BOOK 1d(1) **18 :** the profile of a screw thread

syn FORMALITY, CEREMONY, CEREMONIAL, RITE, RITUAL, LITURGY: FORM is a general word and usu. lacks any special connotation ⟨there had been no fixed order for the coronation of an English king, and the *form* which was observed at Bath was reached only after . . . two experimental drafts —F.M.Stenton⟩ ⟨his inclinations toward the *forms* of the Church of England —G.H.Genzmer⟩ ⟨made his declaration in *form* —Jane Austen⟩ Modified, as by *good* or *bad,* FORM indicates the degree of conformity to established usage or custom ⟨it was accepted poetic good *form* that the lover, writing of his lady, should inventory her charms from top to toe —J.L.Lowes⟩ ⟨nothing could be worse *form* . . . than any display of temper in a public place —Edith Wharton⟩ FORM may indicate a traditional or sanctioned procedure lacking force, significance, or real vitality ⟨if congress remains at liberty to give this court appellate jurisdiction . . . the distribution of jurisdiction made in the Constitution is *form* without substance —John Marshall⟩ FORMALITY applies either to a prescribed procedural detail, often one done perfunctorily and lacking in import, or to an attitude of punctilious, reserved stiffness ⟨the first reading of a public bill is a *formality* and is in effect little more than information given to the House that the bill is on its way —R.M.Dawson⟩ ⟨the cold *formality* of the duchess's court⟩ CEREMONY is likely to suggest dignified, impressive, elaborate, or punctilious performance of actions ranging from those of deep spiritual significance to little everyday courtesies or routine actions ⟨the *ceremonies* at the investiture of a pope⟩ ⟨*ceremonies* in honor of the martyred king⟩ ⟨the beauty of an inherited courtesy of manners, of a thousand little *ceremonies* flowing out of the most ordinary relations and observances of life —Laurence Binyon⟩ CEREMONIAL, occas. a synonym for CEREMONY, is more likely to suggest a system or code of prescribed ceremonies ⟨the gorgeous *ceremonial* of the Burgundian court —W.H.Prescott⟩ RITE indicates the prescribed speech and action of a special formal occasion, esp. a very significant or unusual one, an ordinary event treated as though of major importance, or an esoteric practice ⟨had gone through this formality as resignedly as through all the others which made of a nineteenth century New York wedding a *rite* that seemed to belong to the dawn of history —Edith Wharton⟩ ⟨the semipagan *rites* peculiar to the burial of the dead in middle-class houses —Rudyard Kipling⟩ ⟨abhorred *rites* to Hecate in their obscured haunts —John Milton⟩ RITUAL in its older sense indicates the totality of the rites of service or faith ⟨the Roman *ritual* had always a great attraction for him —Oscar Wilde⟩ More frequently today it designates any series of actions given an unusual importance and a prescribed order or manner ⟨the *ritual* of asepsis today is the same the world over —Harvey Graham⟩ ⟨it was essential to reach a cave around the next headland where she would sit down facing the sea before she thought about anything — thus making a little *ritual* against despair —Audrey Barker⟩ Where it is not an equivalent for RITUAL or RITE, LITURGY may indicate the prescribed form for an act or session of worship as written and accepted ⟨he [Henry VIII] insisted on . . . the maintenance of full ritual in the *liturgy* —Hilaire Belloc⟩

syn FIGURE, SHAPE, CONFORMATION, CONFIGURATION: FORM may suggest an appearance in which both clear outline and also structure and orderly disposition of details are presented or suggested ⟨appearing in book *form*⟩ ⟨the republican *form* of government⟩ ⟨a sense of interdependence and interrelated unity that gave *form* to intellectual stirrings that had been previously inchoate —John Dewey⟩ ⟨school architecture throughout the state is highly specialized. Rigid state laws for heating, ventilation, and lighting offer little opportunity for variation on standard *form* —*Amer. Guide Series: N.J.*⟩ FIGURE is likely to call attention to outlines, to bounding, enclosing circumference or outer lines ⟨a geometrical *figure*⟩ ⟨the *figures* of a dance⟩ ⟨the cloud *figures* in the sky —Sylvia Berkman⟩ ⟨the president rose to his great height, a somber, towering *figure* in black —Sir Winston Churchill⟩ SHAPE may sometimes suggest both outline and also content, mass, body, bulk, or detail ⟨hat *shapes* of beaver, coon, otter, and other skins —*Amer. Guide Series: Conn.*⟩ ⟨the construction of a play sets up its *shape,* and builds its skeleton —John Van Druten⟩ ⟨the *shape* of an idea emerged gradually out of the fog of words —Ellen Glasgow⟩ ⟨whole stone logs are found, some wonderfully and delicately colored, in the *shape* of the Asiatic gingko tree —*Amer. Guide Series: Wash.*⟩ CONFORMATION is usable in reference to whole complicated structure or to detailed arrangement or presentation ⟨they failed to find any relation between altitude tolerance and body stature or *conformation* —H.G.Armstrong⟩ ⟨a culture acquires its *conformation* and specificity from the uniqueness of its institutions —Abram Kardiner⟩ CONFIGURATION is applicable to a detailed outline or statement of the nature and disposition or arrangement of various parts ⟨he used to wake up and not know where he was, but the *configurations* of a dream could easily have taken on such a shape as this — the dining room of the Marlborough in the shadowy light of early morning —Hamilton Basso⟩ ⟨though the main street is wide and lined with stores, most of the others fit crookedly into the *configurations* of the valley —*Amer. Guide Series: Pa.*⟩

Another type of dictionary you should become familiar with is an *unabridged* dictionary. Compare this unabridged definition for the word "form":*

As you see, the definitions in an unabridged dictionary are more complete and informative. Unabridged dictionaries are large volumes, because the entries are longer and include *many* more words than the abridged versions.

EXERCISE A.3   On a sheet of paper, list three specific differences you see as you compare the abridged and unabridged entries:

Where Do You Go if You are Having Trouble Understanding a Dictionary's Format?

Almost all dictionaries, including the little pocket versions, have a "Guide to Using the Dictionary" section near the beginning of the book. This guide will explain the arrangement of the word entries, the various abbreviations used, and provide other information that will help you understand each entry completely.

What Is a Thesaurus?

Another word reference book with which you should become familiar is the *Thesaurus*. *Roget's Thesaurus* was first published in 1852. The *Thesaurus* or treasury of words, is a collection of synonyms, antonyms and other related words. It is named after an English physician, Peter Mark Roget, who had a hobby of making lists of words and grouping them together when they were related to one another.

A thesaurus is *not* a dictionary. It does not *define* words. A thesaurus *can* help you understand what a word means; however, because it provides you with synonyms for each word. By looking at the list of synonyms, you may be able to define the word. Since it lists synonyms, antonyms and other related words, a thesaurus is helpful to have on hand when you are writing. If you find yourself using the same word over and over, and you want to use a different one for variety, look up the word you have been using in the thesaurus to find a synonym.

There are two types of thesauruses available for your use. A standard thesaurus has two parts—an alphabetical index and a text. When you are looking for a word you would first look for that word in the alphabetical index. The information given in the index includes a *keyword* that directs you to the appropriate listing of synonyms in the text.

The type of thesaurus used most frequently by students is the dictionary form. It differs from the standard thesaurus in that there is no index. You look up the word according to alphabetical order, just as if you were using a dictionary. Below is an example of the entry *form*.

> **form**, n. manner, fashion, mode (METHOD); object, thing, phenomenon (VISION); embodiment, cast, conformation (SHAPE); bench, settle (SEAT); class, grade, room (LEARNING).
> **form**, v. fabricate, organize, structure (MAKE-UP); compose make up, constitute (PART); fashion, forge, devise (PRODUCTION); mold, pat, whittle (SHAPE).

> [Source: *Roget's New Pocket Thesaurus in Dictionary Form.* Norman Lewis, Editor. Pocket Books, New York, N.Y. 1972. Page 168.]

There are several ways the information in each entry can be used. Note that the first entry provides synonyms for the word *form* when it is being used as a noun (n). The second entry is for *form* when it is used as a verb (v). The capitalized words in parentheses refer you to other listings or major categories in the book where additional synonyms may be found.

---

*By permission. From WEBSTER'S THIRD NEW INTERNATIONAL DICTIONARY © 1981 by Merriam-Webster, Inc., publisher of the Merriam-Webster ® Dictionaries.

For example, say you were looking for a substitute for the word *form* in the following sentence: "The *form* was moving rapidly toward me." You would first note the word *form* was being used as a noun so you would refer to the first entry. Because you are referring to *form* as a vision or something seen, the thesaurus suggests you could substitute the words *object, thing,* or *phenomenon.* If you didn't care to use one of those, you could also turn to the major category *VISION* for additional listings.

EXERCISE A.4 Use the entries for the word *form* above. On a separate sheet of paper, list possible synonyms you could substitute for *form* in each sentence below.
Example:

One type of thesaurus is written in dictionary *form.*

_____ manner _____   _____ fashion _____   _____ made _____

1. Would you help me *form* my clay for my art project?
2. I would like it to take the *form* of an animal.
3. The score you receive on the test will *form* 50 percent of your final grade.

Check your answers with those found in Appendix B.

As you see, the thesaurus can work very well as a way to learn more about specific words and their relationship to other words. It is also extremely valuable if you are searching for "just the right word" when you are speaking or writing. We suggest that you familiarize yourself with the use of a thesaurus by visiting the library or purchasing an inexpensive paperback version.

What Is a Synonym Finder?

Another reference book we would like to introduce you to is *The Synonym Finder. The Synonym Finder* follows the format of a dictionary. Entries are arranged in alphabetical order and include information such as parts of speech and whether the word is considered slang or not. *The Synonym Finder*'s entry for "form" looks like this:

> **form,** n. 1. configuration, figuration, conformation, formation, arrangement, disposition, organization, order; structure, construction, construct, frame, framework, exterior, outward form.
> 2. figure, physique, build, skeletal structure, body, person; shape, contour, silhouette; appearance, aspect, look, complexion; countenance, visage, feature, face, physiogamy; pose, presence, attitude, bearing, carriage.
> 3. mold, cast, matrix, shaper; pattern, prototype, guide, model; manikin, mannequin, dummy, etc.
> 4. v 10. make, fabricate, manufacture, produce, mint, turn out, put out; construct, build, assemble, set up, put together; erect, elevate, raise, rear, put up.

This is just a part of the actual listening. In all, there are 167 synonyms listed for the word *form.* Included in the list are examples of words no longer found in our vocabulary. Uncommon words such as *limn, formulary,* and *collocate* are also included as synonyms for *form.* Imagine how interesting your paper could be if you varied your vocabulary and used these words.

There are many other reference books being sold that serve the same function and purpose as those we have shared with you. They are all designed to make you knowledgeable and fluent with word usage. These are the sources you should use when you fill out the definition portion of your word cards.

Using Word Structure Clues

Why Should You Learn Greek and Latin?

Do you enjoy puzzles, playing detective, or fitting clues together? If so, you will enjoy working with Greek and Latin roots. Many of our words have come down to us from Greek and Latin, especially terminology relating to medicine, science, and technology. Many are words you use daily such as: bicycle, cent, phonograph. The title of the movie, *E.T., the Extra-Terrestrial,* is an excellent example of how forms of Greek or Latin words are combined to make new words.

Below are examples of Latin prefixes that are often found at the beginning of words:*

Prefix	*Meaning*
ante-	before
con-	against
extra-	outside, beyond
infra-	below, beneath
inter-	between, among
multi-	many, much
nova-	new
pro-	for
super-	above, beyond
trans-	across, over
uni-	one

Other Latin roots and affixes are used to either begin or end a word include:

Roots and Affixes	*Meanings*
agri-, ager	field, farm
cap-	head
card-	heart
cultura-	cultivation
dic(t)-	to say
duc, duct-	to lead
luna-	the moon
man-	hand
mit(t), miss-	to send
natus, nale, nasci-	birth, being born
pend-	to hang
populus, popularis	the people
res, reali-	thing, of things
sanitas	health
Scrib, script-	to write
sonic, sonus	sound
spec(t), spic-	to look
tempo-, tempus	time
terra-	the earth
tract-	to pull
verus, verita(s), verity-	true, truth
vid, vis-	to see

*From Words, Things, Celebrations p. 47.

EXERCISE A.5 Use the above list and on a sheet of paper complete the following:

(1) What is an "extra-terrestrial"?

(2) What might you call a machine that would move across the moon?

(3) What is a *supersonic* airplane?

(4) What is *agriculture*?

(5) Now it's your turn. List 5 words, old or new, formed by combining some of the above Latin roots.

Check your answers with those found in Appendix B.

The Greek language has influenced modern English. Listed below are some of the more common forms, which are usually found at the beginning of words.

Prefixes	Meanings
anti-	against
arch-, arche-	first
auto-	self
ecto-	outside, external
endo-	within, inside
geo-	earth, of the earth
hyper-	over, above
meso-	middle
micro-	small
neo-	new
tele-	far
un-	not

Combining forms that are used to begin or end a word include:

Affixes/Roots	Meanings
anthrop(o)-, anthropy	man, mankind
chronic, chrono-	time
gamos-	marriage
graph-	write
logo-, logy	language, knowledge, study
metro-, metry	measure
morph-	form
philo-, phily	love, love of
phon-	sound
scope-	view
sophy	wisdom, thought
thermo-	heat
toxic, tosico-(a-)	poison

EXERCISE A.6 Use the above lists to answer these questions on a sheet of paper:

1. If you were asked what *chronology* meant, what would you say?

2. Insects are known as *ectomorphs*. Where would you find their skeletons?
3. Humans are *endomorphic*. What do you think this means?

4. List three other words using combinations of the above roots. Make up your own. They may become a part of our language someday!

Check your answers with those found in Appendix B.

Below are listed Greek and Latin roots for numbers:

English	Latin	Greek
one	uni	mono
two	bi, duo	di
three	tri	tri
four	quad, quar	
five	quin	
six	sex, sexi	hex, hexa
seven	sept	
eight	octa, octo, oct	
nine	nov	
ten	deci	dec, deca, deka
hundred	cent	
thousand	mil, mill	
many	multi	poly
half	semi, hemi	hemi
all	omni	span

EXERCISE A.7 Using the above lists of roots and those introduced earlier, answer the following questions on a sheet of paper.

(1) What does the word *cardiology* mean?
(2) What is a *semicircle?*
(3) Since *gamos* means marriage, what is *bigamy?*
(4) A *microscope* comes from what two roots? What do they mean?
(5) What does a *philosopher* do?
(6) An *octopus* has how many legs?
(7) How often do we meet if we meet *biannually?*
(8) How many angles does a *hexagon* have?
(9) What is an *autobiography?* How many roots are used to make this word?

Check your answers with those found in Appendix B.

By knowing Latin and Greek roots you will increase the probability that you will be able to unlock the meaning of an unknown word. Of course, learning roots is only one way to improve your word power.

How Can Words Be Fun?

Up to this point you have been learning vocabulary survival clues. You can use context clues and structural clues (prefix, suffix, roots) to improve, expand, and develop your vocabulary.

Word Histories

Another aspect of vocabulary development is word histories. Our goal is to start you on the way to answering the question: "Where do all these words come from?"
Did you know the following:

The word *honeymoon* comes from ancient times when it was customary for a newly married couple to drink a potion containing *honey* for the first *moon,* or 30 days of their marriage.

Guillotine came from the name of its inventor, Dr. J. I. Guillotine, who thought he was a great humanitarian for inventing a way of death much nicer than the drawnout tortures performed early in history.

The word *galoshes* comes from the royal courts of the French kings. It is a derivation of "galoches," a wooden sandal worn to protect the shoes made of silk and other cloth on wet days.

The popular dog's name *Fido* comes from the Latin word *fidus,* meaning faithful.

Pad as in "I'm going home to my pad" was originally a slang term used by criminals to refer to their bed or jail cell.

Sideburns got their name from a general in the Civil War, General Ambrose Everett Burnside, whose side whiskers became his trademark. They were imitated widely and were first called "burnsides," but the word somehow was switched to "sideburns."

Discovering the origins of words is not only fun and interesting, but often helps us remember a word much longer than if we had just learned a definition.

EXERCISE A.8   Use an unabridged dictionary or word history book. On a sheet of paper, find, record, and share two word histories with your classmates.

What Are Acronyms?

New words are constantly being added to our language. One way this is happening is through the use of *acronyms.* Acronyms are words formed by combining the first letter or syllables of a series of words. Here are some familiar examples.

AWOL	= *A*bsent *W*ithout *O*fficial *L*eave
NABISCO	= *NA*tional *BIS*cuit *CO*mpany
RADAR	= *RA*dio *D*etection *A*nd *R*anging
PREP	= *P*review, *R*ead, *E*xamine, *P*rompt
SCUBA	= *S*elf-*C*ontained *U*nderwater *B*reathing *A*pparatus

How could you use acronyms at school?

EXAMPLE A.16 On a separate sheet of paper match up the following acronyms with their expanded words?

1. _____ ZIP		a.	High Fidelity
2. _____ MASH		b.	Junior College
3. _____ BIOWAR		c.	Situation Normal; All Fouled Up
4. _____ RIF		d.	Aluminum Company of America
5. _____ SEATO		e.	Biological Warfare
6. _____ NASA		f.	Mobile Army Surgical Hospital
7. _____ SNAFU		g.	Congress of Racial Equality
8. _____ ALCOA		h.	Reduction in Force
9. _____ CORE		i.	National Socialist (German National Socialist)
10. _____ NAZI		j.	National Aeronautics and Space Administration
11. _____ JUCO		k.	Zone Improvement Program
12. _____ HIFI		l.	Southeast Asia Treaty Organization

Check your answers with those found in Appendix B.

On a sheet of paper list 5 additional acronyms and their meanings.

Share these with your classmates.

What Are Blends?

Blends are another word form in our language. Blends are formed by taking the beginning portion of one word and combining it with the ending of another or a whole word. One of the best examples of this is the word *smog* which comes from *smoke* and *fog*.

EXERCISE A.10 On a sheet of paper, match the blends listed below with the correct word expansion?

1. _____ albeit		a.	motor hotel
2. _____ Fortran		b.	Boston Red Sox (Baseball team)
3. _____ ballute		c.	medical aid
4. _____ quasar		d.	television broadcast
5. _____ skort		e.	quasi + stellar
6. _____ brunch		f.	formula + translation
7. _____ Bosox		g.	breakfast + lunch
8. _____ Medicaid		h.	shorts + skirt
9. _____ telecast		i.	balloon + parachute
10. _____ motel		j.	twist + whirl
11. _____ twirl		k.	although it be

Check your answers with those found in Appendix B.

Summary

You have been introduced to a method of keeping word cards for new words you come across in your reading. You have learned that there are two aspects to vocabulary development. These are the use of *context clues* and the use of *structure clues*. You have also learned something about how words become a part of our vocabulary.

Building your word power can be an enjoyable and rewarding activity. It is also an activity for you to continue long after you leave your school years behind.

Appendix B
Answer Keys

Chapter 1
Activity 1.2 Getting to Know Your Textbook: Complete the following form for your study skills textbook.

Date _____   Name _____

Textbook Aids

Place a check mark in front of the study aids provided by your text.

✓ Preface or Introduction   ✓ Questions at End of Chapter
✓ Table of Contents   __ Margin Notes
__ Glossary   ✓ Footnotes
__ Subject Index   ✓ Pronunciation Helps for New Terms
__ Author Index   __ Supplemental Lists of Suggested Reading and References
✓ Chapter Introductions   ✓ Charts, Graphs, Diagrams
__ Chapter Pre-reading questions   ✓ Italics, Boldface for Emphasis
✓ Chapter Summaries

How are new terms introduced?

__ bold type   __ margin notes
✓ italics   __ color ink
__ footnotes   __ defined in text
                    __ other

What is the copyright date of the text? <u>1984</u>

Chapter 2
Activity 2.2

7–8 a.m.	Get up, dress, eat, go to work
8–9 a.m.	8:30 begin work, plan day, speak to secretary
9–10	work on Johnson contract; 9:45 work on Good case
10–11	Mrs. Good
11–12	Miss Davis
12–1	12–12:45 lunch 12:45 prepare shoplifting case
1–2 p.m.	1:40 leave for courthouse
2–3	Courthouse
3–4	At Courthouse til 3:30, return to office
4–5	Work on Johnson contract
5–6	Finish up, leave by 5:30 to go home

No time for the Spa unless Miss Davis's appointment does not last an hour

Activity 2.4

	S	M	Tu	W	Th	F	Sa
6–7	sleep						sleep
7–8	get up, get ready, go to school						
8–9		HR	HR	HR	HR	HR	
9–10		Language Arts ---					
10–11		Reading	PE	Reading	PE	Reading	9:30 music
11–12		Math ---					
12–1		eat					
1–2		Science---					
2–3		Social Studies ---					
3–4					3:15 Club		
4–5		4:15 dentist				game	Shopping
5–6		eat ---					Shopping
6–7	music	music	music	music	music	eat	
7–8	math	math	math	lang arts	music		
8–9				soc studies	soc studies	skate	
9–10						skate	
10–11						skate	

Activity 2.6

S	M	Tu	W	Th	F	Sa
				1	2	3
4	5 call airlines	6 noon lunch 12:30	7 call hot line Dallas	8	9 write report	10 carnival 9–1
11 carnival 9–1	12 proof report	13	14 report due	15	16 finish switch	17
18	19 test switch	20	21 start slides	22 prepare	23 for 26th	24
25	26 9:00 meeting	27 write paper Dallas	28	29 finish up slides	30	31

Exercise 2.2 possible reasons

1. The math was easier than Jean anticipated.
2. The civics was a longer assignment than expected.
3. The reading needed to be done more slowly so that all facts could be noted.
4. Jean took too many notes.
5. Jean might have taken longer breaks or been interrupted several times.

Chapter 3
Activity 3.1

A.
1. laughter
2. There was always plenty to make us laugh.
3. We laughedd at many things.

B.
1. Going to court
2. Father kept jumping up from his chair and stabbing the air with his arms, as though he were defending himself before an imaginary jury.
3. Father was nervous and jumped up as if he were practicing before a jury.

C.
1. Boxing match
2. Rocky, you're the world champion.
3. Rocky has won the world championship.

D.
1. Writing from the dictionary
2. Seventh sentence was the way I started copying what eventually became the entire dictionary.
3. Writing from the dictionary helped me to increase my handwriting speed.

Activity 3.2

Main idea: After the French and Indian War, England decided to change the ways in which she treated the colonies.

1. England felt the colonies needed more protection from the Indians
2. The war left England with a large debt
3. England believed the colonies did not have enough respect for English law

Activity 3.3

1) b   2) a   3) Answers could include:

The male carries the eggs
The seahorse sucks food into its mouth
It can wrap its tail around a piece of seaweed to stay still

Chapter 4
Activity 4.1

A. This article centers around fire fighters and how they fight and put out forest fires in the United States.
B. This article gives the background and importance of how coins were developed in Early America.
C. The story discusses Brother Matthias of St. Mary's Industrial Home for Boys and his influence on Babe Ruth and their love for baseball.
D. The characteristics of a successful, professional salesperson.
E. The story talks about the effects that certain colors have on people.

Activity 4.2

A. 1. This article discusses ways people can take care of their pets.
   2. Answers could include knowing about the pet's diet, exercise pattern, and responsibility of taking care of the pet.
   3. Answer could include learning about the background of the pet, what to do when the pet is sick, and how to train the pet.
B. 1. The article shows how to read and understand a road map in order to help you get to where you want to go.
   2. Basic information could include knowing the major and minor roads, locating cities, and directions (N, S, E, W) on the map.
   3. This could include determining the mileage between the cities, the different time zones and identifying the interstate highway system.
C. 1. This article discusses the contributions that the Congress Wagon made in the development of America.
   2. The Conestoga Wagon was the one that the pioneers used to haul freight and traveled in to the West.
   3. New information could include learning the history of the Conestoga Wagon, how it was built, the dimensions, and why it was so valuable to the pioneers.
D. 1. This story is about an auto race from Peking, China, to Paris, France.
   2. The race was long and there were many dangers.
   3. Answer could include who were the participants, what year did they race, how long did it take, and what were some of the interesting experiences.
E. 1. Thunderstorms and what effect they have on the weather.
   2. Thunderstorms can cause a lot of damage, help to form tornados, and yield a lot of rain in a short period of time.
   3. When, where, why, and how thunderstorms are formed and what to do in a severe storm.

Activity 4.3

1. The percentage of time during the day a student spends sleeping, playing, eating, watching TV, and school activities.
2. The student spends 48 percent of the time eating and playing, and another 33 percent sleeping. Only 25 percent is spent in school and related activities.
3. Sleeping and eating

Activity 4.4

Check on this.
The ideas could include these questions:

1. What does a cheetah look like?
2. Why is the cheetah called an "Earthbound Flier?"
3. Why is the cheetah so fast?

Activity 4.5

The ideas could include these questions:

1. What is "Malarkey's Arky?"
2. Where did "Malarkey's Arky" come from?
3. Is "Malarkey's Arky" similar to a boat?

Activity 4.6

1. An outline of the development of human flight from the beginning to present day.
2. 4
3. Gliders
   The Wright Brothers and other Pioneers
4. c
5. Heavier-than-Air Flight

Exercise 4.1

1. Answers will vary
2. The different methods by which seeds get from one place to another (flying, floating, exploding, hitchhiking)
3. Information could include: how certain seeds travel through the air, and how birds, and people spread seeds.

   Second

1. The different methods that seeds can travel.
2. Seeds travel to different places by flying, floating, exploding, hitchhiking, birds and people.
3. Information could include the different methods of how seeds travel, why it is important to have traveling seeds, when and where do seeds travel.

   Third

1. What two methods do seeds travel?
2. What is the author discussing in the article?
3. What can you conclude about seeds that travel?
4. What did you think of the author's organization of the article?
5. In what ways can traveling seeds benefit the environment?

*Other questions will vary from the above

Chapter 5
Activity 5.1

Recall Column	Note Column
	Contact Lens
	Advantages of contact lenses
	—CL are convenient, safe
	—CL moves as the eye moves
	—CL do not fog up, get wet or dirty
	—Many people wear them who depend on accurate vision
	Psychological benefits of contact lenses
	—people feel they look better
	—myopia is usually controlled by contact lenses people do not have to wear thick lenses.
	—people can become more involved
	Contact lenses have many uses
	—change the color of a person's eyes
	—to create special effects
	—to correct vision problems
	Summary:

Exercise 5.0

1. What does a mollusk look like?
2. How does a mollusk move about?
3. What is the relationship between a mollusk and an echinoderm?

Exercise 5.1

1. What are the major uses for aspirin as indicated in the article?
2. Why is it necessary to continue to do research on aspirin?

Exercise 5.2

1. What are 3 advantages of a computer?
2. How can the computer be used in the home?
3. How can the computer be applied to school work?

Exercise 5.3

Waves in the ocean can become very big. Some of the largest waves in the world can be found near the tip of South America. When you see a wave the water hardly moves. This is because waves are movements which happen under the water.

Exercise 5.4

Water picks up loose soil and debris and moves it great distances from the mountains. The more rapidly water flows the more soil and rocks that can be moved. In this process, the heavier particles are the first to settle to the bottom, the lighter particles stay in suspension and settle when the water slows down. Water erodes stream banks and carries material downstream. How much and how far material is carried depends on how rapidly the water is moving.

Activity 5.2

a. The beast put his paw on the little creature and would have killed it.
b. Lincoln spent less than a year in school. He worked first for his father, then for neighboring farmers.
c. Lincoln cleared brush, chopped trees, plowed, pulled fodder, husked corn. He did all types of work as long as he had a book and a chance to read.
d. People see more meteors between midnight and sunrise than sunset and midnight.
e. Man learned to tame and raise animals to provide meat, milk, hides and wool and also to make butter and cheese.

Activity 5.3

Recall	Notes
	Study of Matter
	Matter
What's Matter?	—anything that has mass and occupies space
	examples are stars, planets, rocks, water, all living things
	Elements
How many elements?	—the basic materials of our world.
	88 elements have been found on earth in the natural state
	these elements can be combined to form new combinations
An atom is?	Atom is the smallest unit of an element
	Atom is chemically the same as the other atoms of that element
	Atoms are too small to be seen
	X-rays are used to determine the size and shape of an atom
	Atomic Structure
Explain a proton, electron, neutron, nucleus	proton—a positive charge
	electron—a negative charge
	neutron—no charge
Describe an electron cloud	nucleus—protons and neutrons form the center electrons move outside the nucleus
	atom is electrically neutral when number of electrons = the number of protons in the nucleus
	energy level is where an electron is found at any one time
	electron cloud is all the energy levels together

Summary

Matter is anything that occupies mass and spaces. Elements are the basic material of our world. The smallest part of an element is an atom. Its size and shape can be determined by the use of X-ray. A nucleus consists of protons and neutrons. Electrons move outside the nucleus. An electron cloud consists of all the energy levels which is the area where an electron is usually found at any one time.

Recall	Notes
What is history?	*The Study of History*
	History
	is the study of the past. A scholar is a learned person. A historian is one who knows a lot about history.
	Human Race
What are the characteristics of the human race?	Humans share the same ancestors. Human race is one species—called homo sapien. People can think, are able to invent things. People can develop languages, share ideas and pass them on to others.
	Importance of History
	tells us how we came to be the way we are
	Without history we would have lost what our ancestors discovered and learned.
Why is history important?	legends are stories about the past.
	new discoveries are being made all the time
	to help us learn more about our past.
	Summary
	History is the study of the past. Historians are people who know a lot about history. Modern man shares the ideas of our ancestors which include thinking, inventing, or discovering new things and communicating through language.
	History helps us to understand how we came to be.
	New discoveries help us appreciate and understand our past. The goal of this book is to read about what is important to us today.

Chapter 7
Exercise 7.0

1) F	3) F	5) T
2) F	4) F	

Exercise 7.1

1) b	3) a	5) d
2) b	4) c	

Exercise 7.2

1. Knowing how to study provides you with a plan that will increase your confidence and productivity. It will help you develop better study habits and make learning easier. It will help you to become a better student.
2. A flexible reader is one who realizes and understands that all materials are not read at the same rate. A flexible reader will also choose the reading rate best for the material. A flexible reader adjusts the rate and the purpose for reading to the material.
3. The PREP Study System represents a systematic approach for putting information into long-term memory. The four major parts are:
   1. Previewing—getting an overview of the material.
   2. Reading actively—becoming involved with the material, taking notes, mapping, and asking yourself questions about the material you have read.
   3. Examining—asking and answering questions about the material after you have gotten your notes.
   4. Prompting—using memory skills and techniques to help you recall the material.
   Using the PREP Study System will help you become a more effective reader, learn more, and understand more fully what you are reading.
4. Notetaking is recording the most important ideas from a lecture or textbook. The notetaking system consists of the notes, a recall column, and a summary statement at the end of the notes.
      Mapping is a pictorial representation of your notes. Notetaking and mapping are similar because they both list the most important ideas and thoughts. The major difference is that mapping is a graphic representation of the material, while notetaking is notes, a recall column, and summary.

Exercise 7.3

Questions might be:

Sleeping Gear:

1. Down filled sleeping bags are not as good as polyester-filled sleeping bags. (F)
2. The main idea of this passage was:
   a. backpackers and their sleeping gear   (a) is the answer.
   b. sleeping gear
   c. ground cover for sleeping
   d. advantages of a polyester filled sleeping bag
3. If you were going backpacking, what type of gear would you want to have for the trip?

Backpackers' sleeping gear usually consists of a sleeping bag, a foam pad or air mattress, a waterproof ground cover, and a water resistant cover. Foam pads are usually preferred to air mattress because they are easier to use and will not go flat during the night. The best sleeping bag is down filled. The polyester filled sleeping bag is also good. In backpacking, it is necessary to have the right equipment.

Questions might be:

Sharks:

1. Most of the sharks are fish eaters (T)
2. "Feeding frenzy" is described as:
   a. following a ship for handouts
   b. eating logs or anything the sharks can grab
   c. dining on fish, turtles, seals
   d. becoming excited over their meal   (d) is the answer.
3. What types of food do sharks live on?

 Sharks are mainly fish eaters even though they have been known to eat clams, mussels, seals, turtles, and other sharks. Sometimes sharks become so excited when they are eating that they will eat anything they can grab. This includes logs, propellors, and anything else close to them.

Questions might be:

Smoke Jumpers:

1. One way to break the fire triangle is to remove the fuel from the triangle.
2. The smoke jumper's job is to:
   a. Bring in more equipment
   b. Use the proper equipment
   c. Break the fire triangle   (c) is the answer.
   d. Be in the right place to fight the fire
3. What is a fire triangle and when is a fire triangle broken? A fire triangle consists of three sides, heat, fuel, and air. When one of these is removed, the triangle is broken and the fire goes out.

Questions might be:

Bush Pilot:

1. Sheldon's main job is flying groups of mountain climbers to their base camp and delivering supplies to them. (T)
2. One of the characteristics a bush pilot does *not* have is:
   a. making the repair on his own plane
   b. courage
   c. being able to survive in all kinds of weather if he is found down
   d. a desire to expose the passengers to danger (d) is the answer.
3. What qualities of a bush pilot were described in the passage?
    A bush pilot is a special kind of pilot. The pilot must have courage, know the area and landmarks. The pilot must be able to make repairs on the airplane. Also the pilot must know good survival skills and be an excellent pilot who can fly in all kinds of weather.

Exercise A.1

1) note = write
2) diffuse = spread
3) goiter = a swelling
4) replicate = do it again
5) legible = easy to read
6) perennial = living longer than one season

Exercise A.2

1) Latin
2) 3, noun, verb (transitive and intransitive)
3) number 4

Exercise A.3

Answers will vary; should include longer entry.

Exercise A.4

1) mold, pat, whittle
2) embodiment, cast, conformation
3) compose, make-up, devise

Exercise A.5

1) outside the earth
2) lunar
3) beyond the speed of sound (supersonic)
4) farm cultivation (agriculture)
5) answers will vary

Exercise A.6

1) chronology = language, knowledge, study of time
2) ectomorph = outside the form
3) endomorphic = inside the form (body)
4) answers will vary

Exercise A.7

1) cardiology = study of the heart
2) semicircle = half a circle
3) bigamy = 2 or more marriages at one time
4) microscope = What two roots?
   a) micro = small
   b) scope = view
5) philosopher = thinks
6) octopus = eight
7) twice a year
8) six
9) autobiography = a story a person writes about himself/herself

Exercise A.8

Answers will vary.

Exercise A.9

1. k
2. f
3. e
4. h
5. l
6. j
7. c
8. d
9. g
10. i
11. b
12. a

Exercise A.10

1. k
2. f
3. i
4. e
5. h
6. g
7. b
8. c
9. d
10. a
11. j

A-1 CHANGING WEATHER

1. *Cirrus clouds* are white. They are shaped like a feather. *Stratus clouds* form a layer across the sky. They look like fog. *Cumulus clouds* are thick and puffy. Most have flat bottoms. The tops are rounded like hills. When dark, they contain rain.
2. Water from a lake or ocean or others is heated by the sun and evaporates into the air as water vapor. When the vapor is cooled, it turns back into water drops. This is called condensation. These drops collect together to make clouds. When the water drops get too heavy, they fall from the cloud as rain. The rain falls back to earth and the cycle can begin again.
3. Answers will vary.

Vocabulary Exercise

1) c
2) d
3) b
4) b
5) a
6) b
7) c

A-2 BUSH PILOTS IN GLACIER LAND

1. A bush pilot has to be able to refuel, change the oil and repair his own plane. The pilot must be able to fly in snowstorms without landmarks to follow. He must know how to survive if he has to make a forced landing somewhere away from civilization.
2. Bush pilots take the place of these other transportation systems and carry food, supplies and mail to different parts of the state that are not reachable any other way.
3. A bush pilot receives the same kind of flight training any pilot receives. They also need to learn how to be an airplane mechanic, so they can fix their own planes. They also need to be very familiar with the instruments in their plane as they sometimes might be flying in heavy snowstorms and will not be able to see the land they are flying over and will have to rely on instruments to navigate.

Vocabulary Exercise

1) c
2) a
3) d
4) b
5) b
6) a
7) a

A-3 FRANKLIN THE SCIENTIST

1. The colonists thought the stamp act was unfair because the colonists would have to pay extra money on everything that was sold.
2. a) Franklin went to Great Britain and persuaded the King to remove the Stamp Act. b) He talked France into sending aid to help America become an independent nation from Great Britain. c) He helped write the Declaration of Independence.
3. Franklin helped lay the groundwork of the United States through writing the Declaration of Independence. He also assisted the United States in becoming an independent, free nation. The lightening rod that Franklin developed still protects homes and barns from fire today.

Vocabulary Exercise

1) b
2) a
3) b
4) b
5) c
6) a
7) b

A-4 THE GREEK WAY OF LIFE

1. Zeus was the father and ruler of all the gods.
2. Sparta was considered a military city because all the boys were trained as soldiers. The boys left home at 7 and lived in special camps. All the men ate together, exercised together and learned to suffer pain.
3. Both are ruled by the people. Women are free in our country but were not as free in Greece. They couldn't vote in Greece. Greeks owned slaves but that is against the law here. We have elected representatives to the House and Senate but all free men could vote and be in the Greek assembly. Both elect the highest officials. In both Greece and the U.S. men can serve in the courts of the law.

Vocabulary Exercise

1) b
2) c
3) c
4) a
5) c
6) b
7) a

A–5 HOW TO READ A ROAD MAP

1. A road map legend shows the different symbols and marks that appear on the map and explains what each of these marks stands for. Road map legends help you understand the language of a map. Legends can show you how to find campgrounds, parks, historical monuments and recreation areas. They also show you how to find out if a highway is a freeway, an expressway, or an unpaved road.
2. The author wrote this article to help people realize how valuable a good navigator can be when you are taking a trip in an automobile. She wrote the article to help people understand how easy it is to read a road map and be a good navigator if they are a passenger in a car. It also helped explain the correct way to read a road map.
3. The most important thing you need to take is a good map. You also would want to take a flashlight to help you read the map in the dark. A magnifying glass would help you see all the little markings on the map. You should also take colored pens to mark your route out on the map.

Vocabulary Exercise

1) a
2) d
3) c
4) c
5) b
6) a
7) b

A–6 WHAT MAKES FOOD SPOIL?

1. Warm and damp environment assist the microorganisms to grow.
2. Dampness and warmth are conditions that encourage microorganisms to grow. When microbes eat and digest the food, they produce wastes that can cause an odor, molds, or a scum which results in food becoming spoiled.
3. Foods can be refrigerated, canned, salted, dried, and frozen. Periodic health examinations for workers can be given so that germs or disease will not be spread through the handling of food.

Vocabulary Exercise

1) d
2) b
3) c
4) b
5) d
6) b
7) d

A–7 EUROPEANS ARRIVE IN THE MIDDLE COLONIES

1. The King of England owed money to Penn's father, Admiral Penn. William tried to collect it after his father's death but the King wouldn't pay. The King gave land to Penn instead of the money.
2. The Quakers had no preacher. Everyone was allowed to speak. They believed all men were created equal. They did not believe in war. They did not swear loyalty to the King.
3. The Dutch West Colony India Colony was founded to trade furs with the Indians and to settle the land explored by Hudson. Colonists left from it to make settlements along the Hudson River.

Vocabulary Exercise

1) b
2) d
3) a
4) c
5) a
6) c
7) d

A–8 THE CAMEL'S SECRET

1. The camels were not given any water or any food with water in it. The scientists monitored the temperature and humidity in the air the animals breathed by putting a sensor in the nostrils of the camels. When the camels started to dehydrate and lose weight, they started exhaling cooler and drier air than they did normally.

2. The camel's body is well insulated and doesn't react to temperature changes as much as a human's body. The camel doesn't have a need to perspire as much and it also has kidneys that retain water. A camel also doesn't lose very much water when it exhales when it is conserving. Conservation just means that the camel's body conserves water when it is hot and thirsty.

3. When it is hot out, animals and humans lose a lot of water by perspiring. We also lose a lot of water when we exhale because warm air contains more water vapor than cool air. The body tells us that it needs to replace water when we are thirsty.

Vocabulary Exercise

1) a
2) c
3) b
4) c
5) d
6) c
7) a

A–9 ENERGY FOR THE FUTURE

1. One fifth of the world's coal is found in the United States.

2. Plants and animals that were living in the hot steamy swamps 300 million years ago died and rotted. More plants then grew on top of them, died, rotted, and formed a thick solution which is called peat. Beneath the swamps, the earth shifted. Water, mud, and sand then rushed in to fill the low places. Through the weight of the water and mud, along with years of time and pressure, the peat hardened into rock which today is called coal.

3. The supply of oil may run out. Imported oil can become very expensive. Spilled oil can kill birds, fish, and other animals when the oil gets into the rivers, lakes, and oceans as well as turning beaches black and sticky.

Vocabulary Exercise

1) d
2) a
3) c
4) b
5) b
6) a
7) d

A–10 THE CALIFORNIA GOLD RUSH

1. Most goods had to be brought by ship all the way from the East around South America's Cape Horn to San Francisco. Then the goods were hauled to the fields by boat, wagon, muleback and even people. Each person handling the goods made a profit. Then the store owners added more to the price so they could make a profit too.

2. New settlements sprang up. Great numbers of people came to California. More roads were made. Prices were very high for most all goods. Living conditions were crude. There were very few things a miner could do for fun. In later years women and actors came to entertain in the theatres. A great amount of money was made from the gold.

3. Answers will vary.

Vocabulary Exercise

1) a
2) c
3) d
4) d
5) b
6) b
7) b

A-11 TAKING THE EARTH'S PULSE

1. Surface and body waves.
2. An earthquake is a trembling of the ground.
3. This information assists the scientist in determining how severe an earthquake is by ranking it on the Richter or Mercalli scale.

Vocabulary Exercise

1) b
2) a
3) d
4) d
5) b
6) c
7) b

A-12 A PRIMER FOR BABYSITTERS

1. The author said that two-year-olds are very active and need to be watched at all times. They like to unlock doors and to experiment with taking things apart and putting them together again. The best kind of toys for them to play with are toys they can pull apart and put back together. Keep two-year-olds away from electrical appliances and matches and lighters. Two-year-olds also like to climb, so cupboards should be free of things that might hurt or poison them.
2. This article was written for anyone that babysits children. It describes the different things to watch for with each age child up to seven years of age. It also gives suggestions for things babysitters can do with the different age children.
3. It would be fun to take a four-year-old to a park where you could play ball or climb on playground equipment. If it was raining we could play school and I would bring paints, coloring books, paper and scissors and maybe a chalkboard and chalk.

Vocabulary Exercise

1) b
2) a
3) a
4) d
5) a
6) c
7) b

142